The Untamed Sea

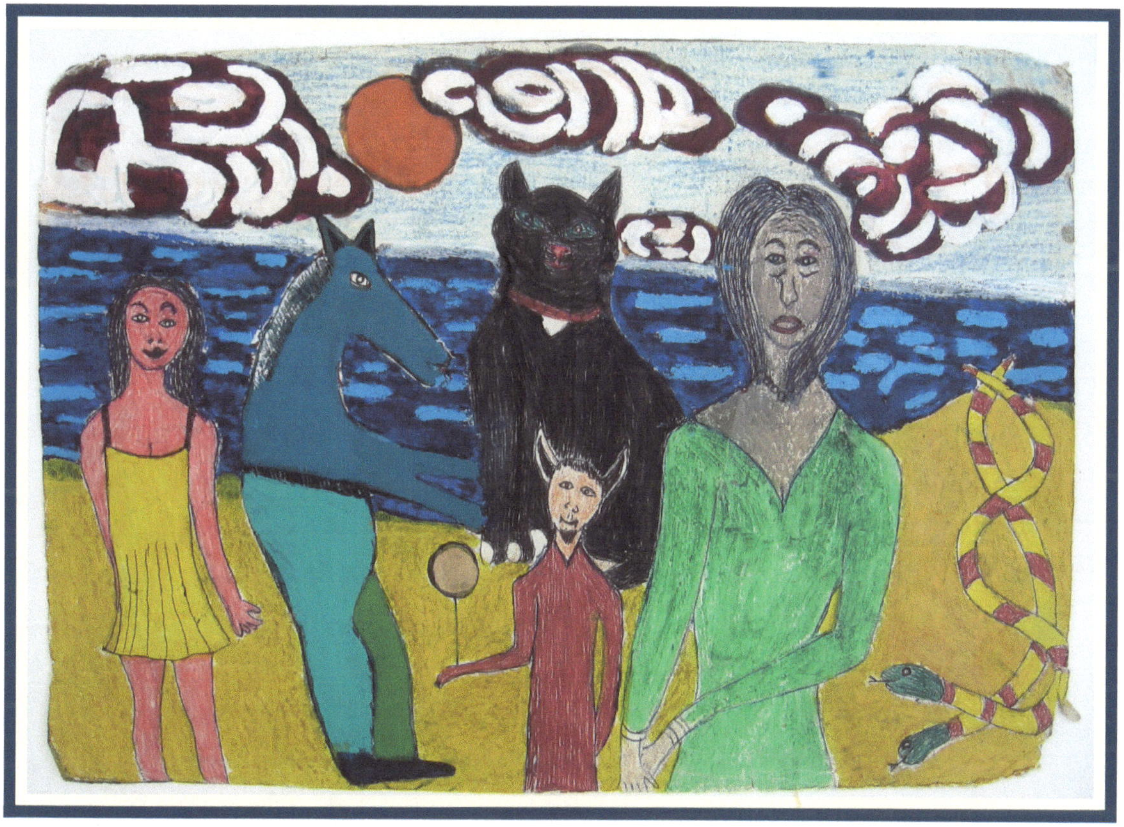

Paintings by Ronald Q Henriques

Insider Art (Publishing) Ltd.

PO Box 272. Exeter. EX2 9ZL

www.insiderart.org.uk

ISBN 978-0-9553400-4-8

Set in Tahoma 10pt

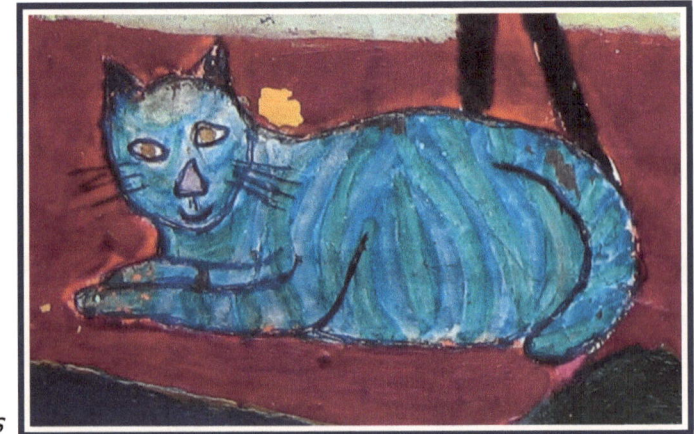

Detail: A Man for All Seasons

The Untamed Sea

Paintings by Ronald Q Henriques

Edited by Malcolm Learmonth & Karen Huckvale

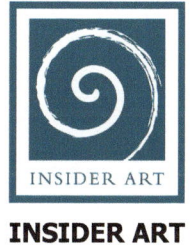

INSIDER ART

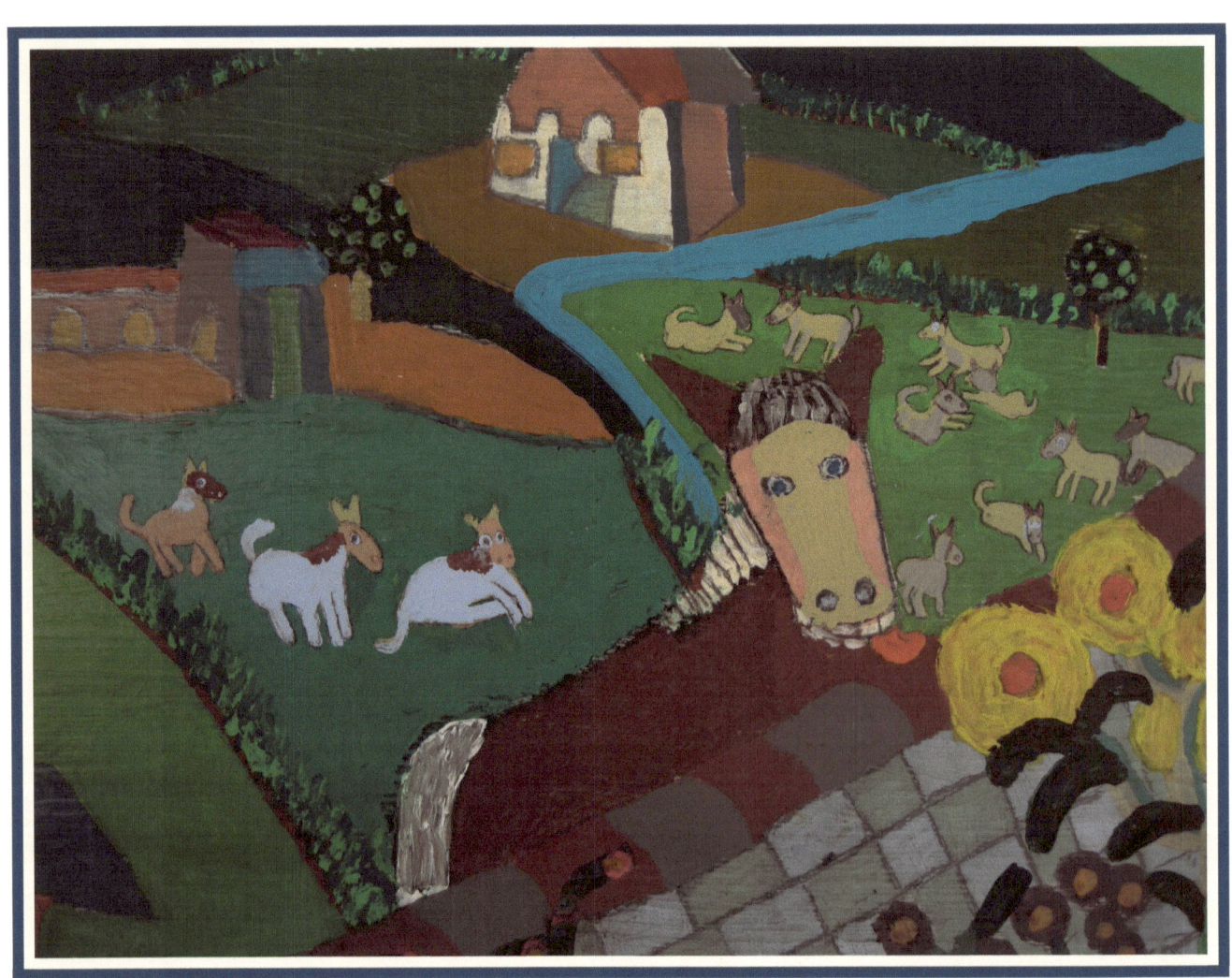

Detail: Geographic Event.

CONTENTS

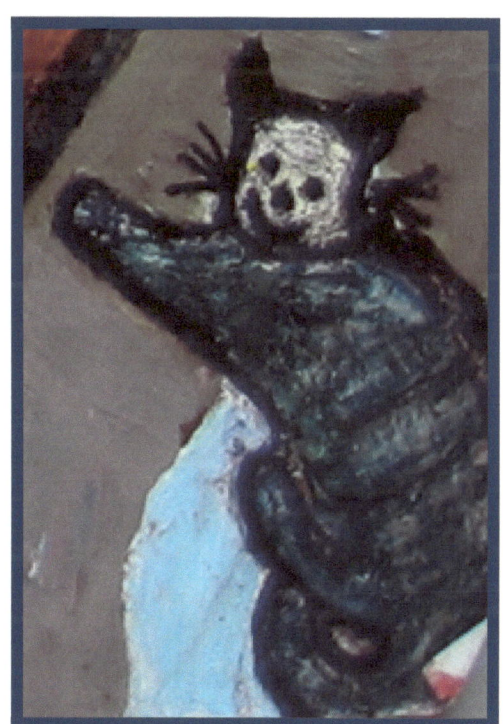

Detail: A Day in the Box

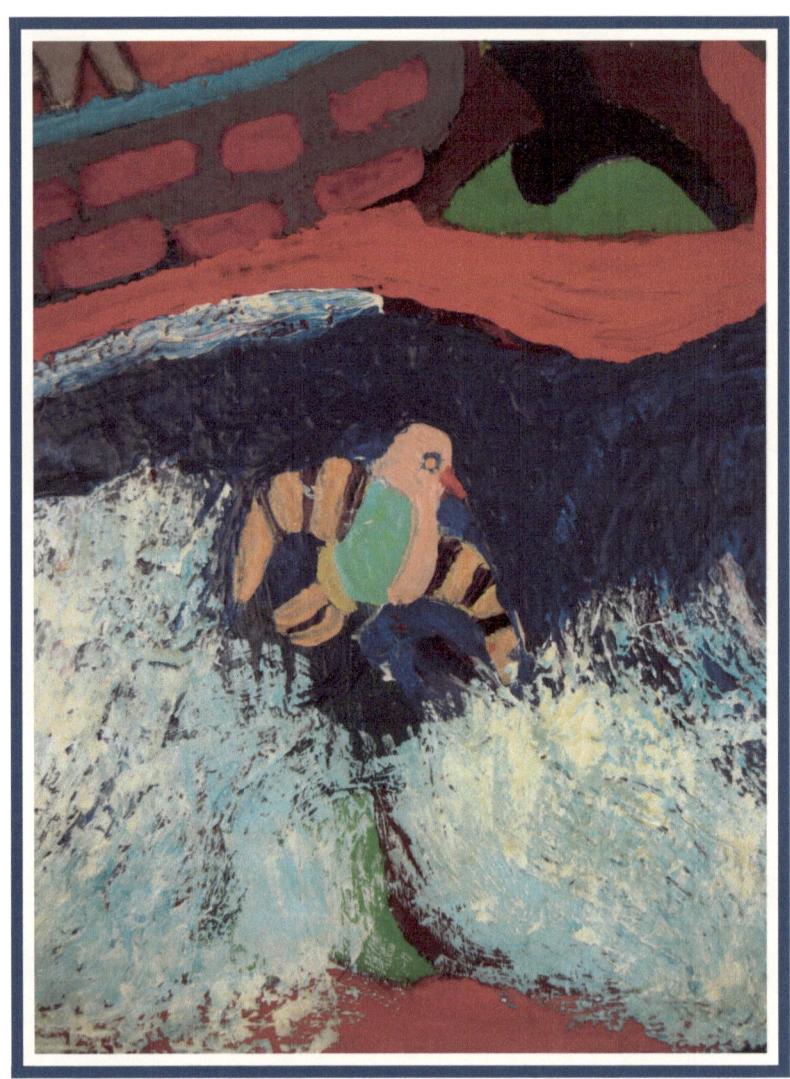

Detail: The Lazy Sailor.

SERIES INTRODUCTION

This volume is the third print publication from Insider Art, following *Love, Desire and Teen Spirit: Reflections on the Dynamic Force of Adolescent Eros* by Joolz McLay in 2009, and *A Jungian Circumambulation of the Arts and Therapy: Ornithology for the Birds* by Michael Edwards in 2010.

It is the nature of both art and psychotherapy to be 'liminal': to be 'boundary dwelling'. Both imply journeys between inner and outer, rigour and spontaneity, past, present and future, relationship and identity. Art therapy, as a combination of these liminalities, inevitably amplifies them. So explorations of the field and the habitats that surround it do not always fit neatly into categories. The series is a search for what connects, as well as for what differentiates. This sense of the spaces between as ones of fascination and fertility, and not without complexity and difficulty, is amplified even more when art therapy comes into contact with work like the paintings in this book.

Malcolm Learmonth & Karen Huckvale.
Series Editors.

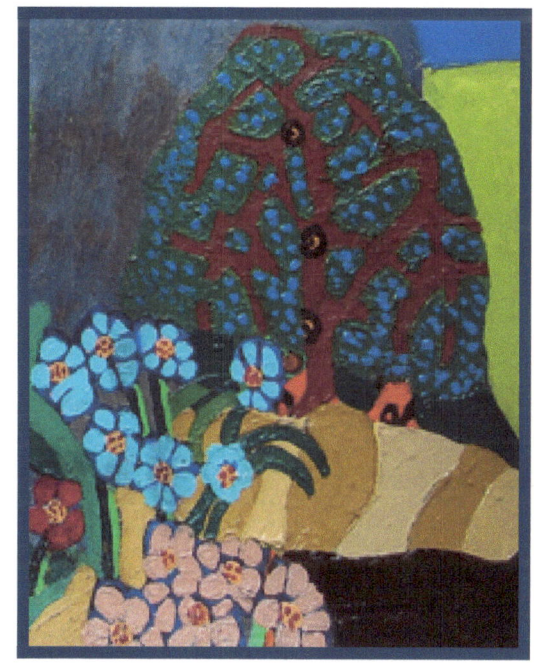

Detail: Far from the Madding Crowd

About the Artist

Ronald was born in 1949 in Wuppertal, West Germany where his father was serving with the British Army on the Rhine. The family – Ronald's two sisters, his father and his mother who was Dutch - moved to England in Ronald's early years, and eventually settled in Surrey to life on a farm. Ronald liked the peace of nature and the animals, images of which can be seen in his work.

Having attended a local school, Ronald went on to Frensham Heights School as a boarder. He hadn't wanted to leave home and feels he didn't make use of what the school had to offer in the way of education and sociability.

During late adolescence Ronald lived at home attending further education, working, or writing his book 'The Circus of Simon Hollander'. He then spent some time at Brookwood Hospital in Surrey and remembers it as being very frightening and daunting.

Ronald moved with his mother and father to Kenn just outside Exeter in 1972, then spent a long time at Digby hospital which he describes as having been a frightening and disturbing experience. During this time he wrote and worked increasingly on his drawing and painting.

From Digby Ronald moved to Spurfield House in Exminster where he continued to paint, and in the late 1990's his cousin Veronica Gosling exhibited his paintings at her gallery, 'The Barn at Hay Farm' in the Forest of Dean.

Over recent years Ronald's work has been exhibited at several venues in Exeter including The Phoenix Bar and at the Exeter Arts and Therapies conferences - with support from Insider Art - and also at Gallery 36 – established by his cousin Veronica on moving to Exeter.

Ronald now lives in Exeter and has a studio at EVA Studios, an artist's co-operative in Alphington.

Ronald says about his work:

'My first serious art piece was while I was in an asylum. It was a way of getting out of the hospital rather like climbing a high brick wall. I started painting in the 1980's, when I was going through a hard time, and because of this the paintings of that time are particularly vivid. I was in a frightening situation and was ultra-perceptive.

My original paintings depicted a combination of thoughts and experiences. They are quite varied – there is a theme that occurs that I'm trying to trace, sometimes subjects recur, maybe from artificial landscapes. My later paintings are more decorative and skilled as an intention.

My eventual aims are to develop some sort of evidence of myself, exploring situations more and more and developing a more professional application of paint as an artist. I'd like to cross a frontier from semi expressionism to more figurative. I'd like to enjoy painting and be even more creative.'

Ronald's vivid paintings are highly personal and imaginative, demonstrating a skillful sense of composition. He uses mainly acrylics, but also experiments with other materials such as pastels, crayons or spray-on gold. He does not always like to sell his originals, but his work lends itself very well to prints.

As well as his painting, Ronald loves listening to music, and has always been interested in astronomy and for a long time also in photography. His photographs provide a fascinating record of his experiences and of the people around him and show the same well-developed sense of composition that can be seen in his paintings. He thinks about how to make life easier and better for people and has over 500 ideas for different inventions.

Ronald hopes to send this book overseas to be enjoyed by a wider audience.

By Jenny Henriques, Veronica Gosling & Ronald Henriques. January 2012

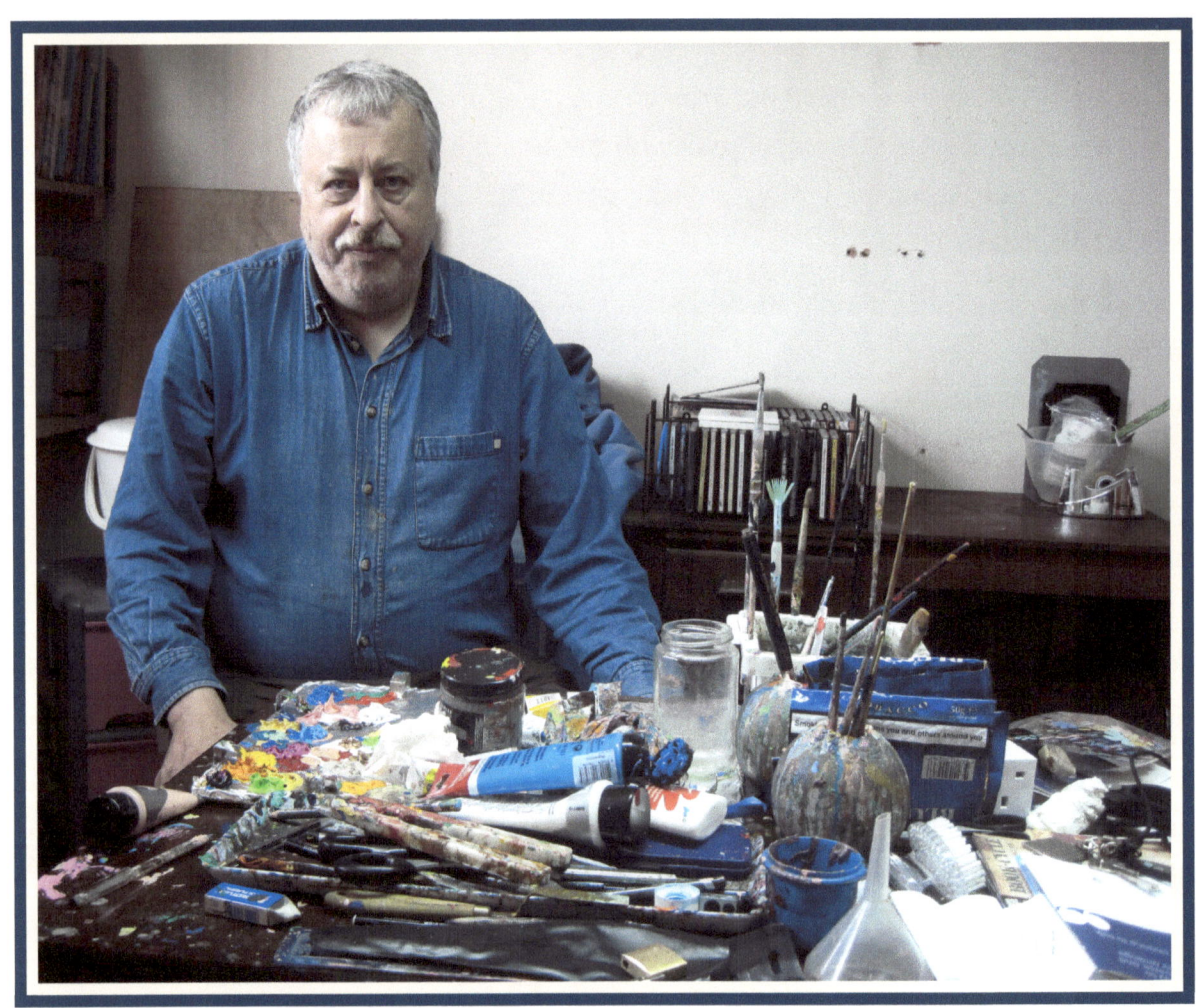

Ronald Quixano Henriques

Introduction

I met Ronald Henriques nearly 15 years ago. I was asked to meet him in my professional capacity as an art psychotherapist. Ronald was a long term user of mental health services in and around Exeter in the South West of England. I was told in advance that Ronald painted and that it would be a good idea to meet him where he was living, rather than invite him to my art therapy room, because then I would see more of his work.

I was taken aback by the richness and quantity of the work, and took a liking to this courteous and gentle man. It was clear to me very quickly that psychotherapy as such was not what would be helpful. What Ronald really seemed to appreciate was my interest in, and appreciation of, his paintings. My job of course is not to be an art critic, curator or collector. It is to support people's mental health. The paintings were so clearly central to Ronald's life that this did not present a conflict: supporting and encouraging his 'artist' identity was in itself a contribution to the artist's well-being.

With this in mind I have regularly visited Ronald, talked about painting with him, helped to organise shows of his work, and studio space for him, projects wholeheartedly supported by Ronald's family and many people in Devon Partnership NHS Trusts Recovery and Independent Living service,

Ronald finds it hard to sell paintings themselves. This is partly because he often wants to return to pieces, sometimes over many years, and rework, or as he calls it 'refurbish' them. For this reason we have made no attempt to date or sequence the work. I personally have not always felt that these refurbishments are actually improvements aesthetically and it is this sort of issue that brings into focus the basic question of whether one is working in service of well-being or of art. I have no doubt that the refurbishment is part of an ongoing and living relationship between the artist and the images, and that it would be deeply unhelpful to attempt to interfere with this conversation. Perhaps art making is always, on one level, a conversation between the inner and outer life and some varieties of mental health issues make the boundary between them more permeable than it is for many of us.

It is a privilege to be able to publish Ronald's paintings in book form leaving the artists conversation with the originals to grow in peace. Nevertheless share the extraordinarily imagination, sheer hard work, persistence, commitment, and unique vision that Ronald's work embodies. All of Ronald's work is mixed media with acrylic paint being the predominant medium. He works on paper, cardboard and hardboard. Most paintings are approximately A1 (23" x 33") in size. Ronald's generous use of varnish sometimes makes his work very hard to photograph but the varnish is very much part of the work. Some of the older pieces have been so worked and handled over many years that their edges are frayed. This too becomes part of their patina and several have been photographed deliberately so as to not exclude this tangibility of their ongoing inner life.

Malcolm Learmonth 2012

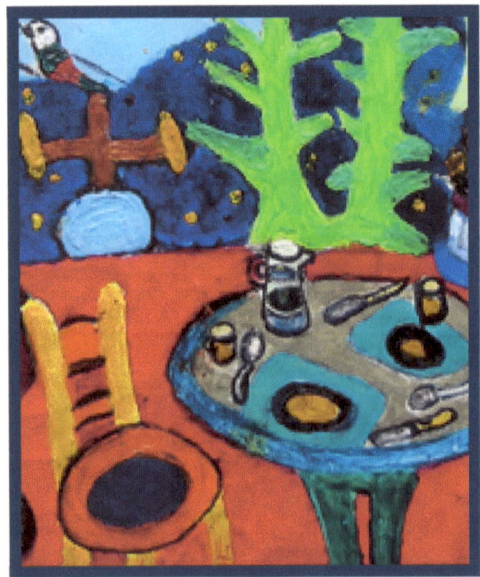

Detail: A Day in the Box

The Paintings

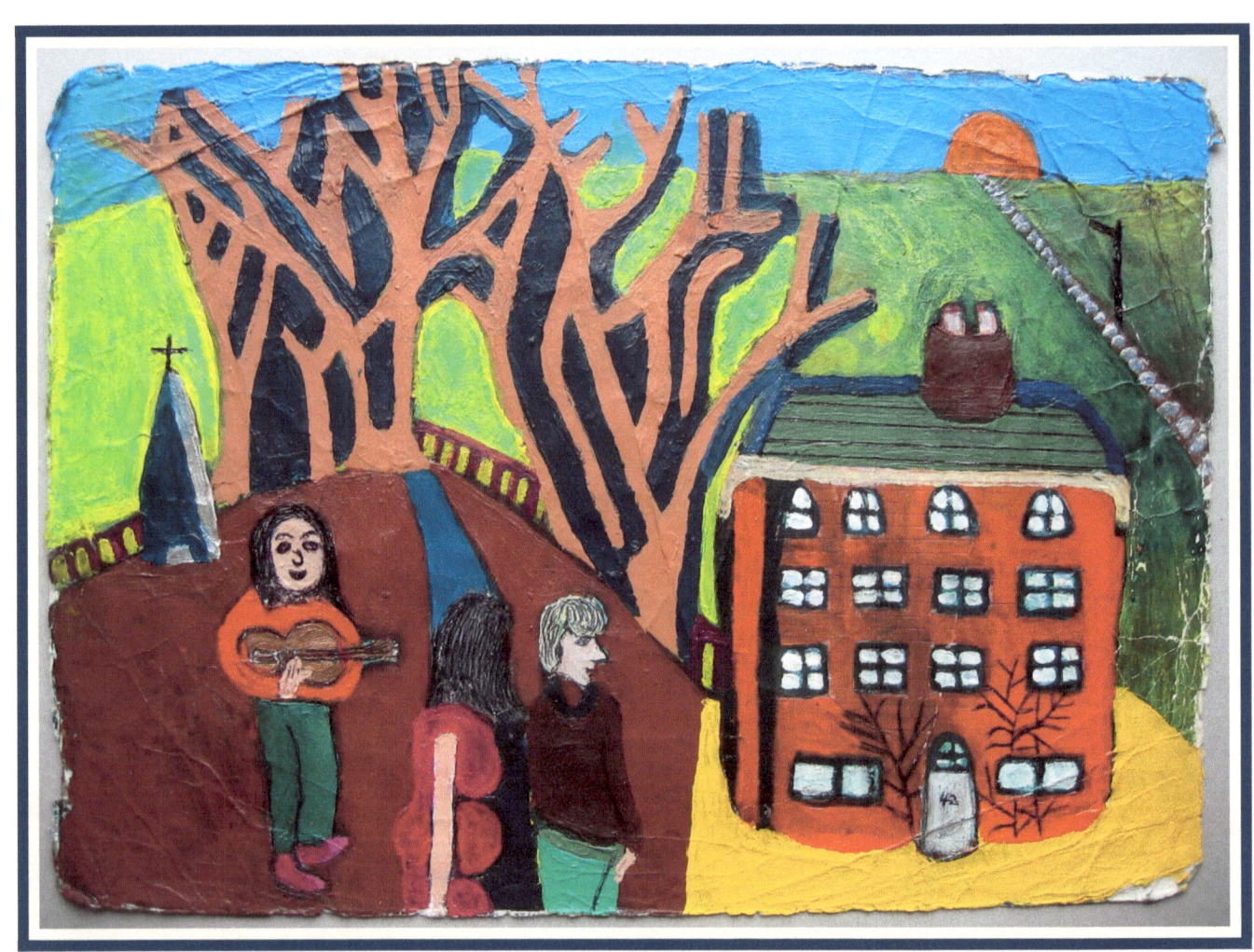

The Doctors Own Medicine. Mixed media.

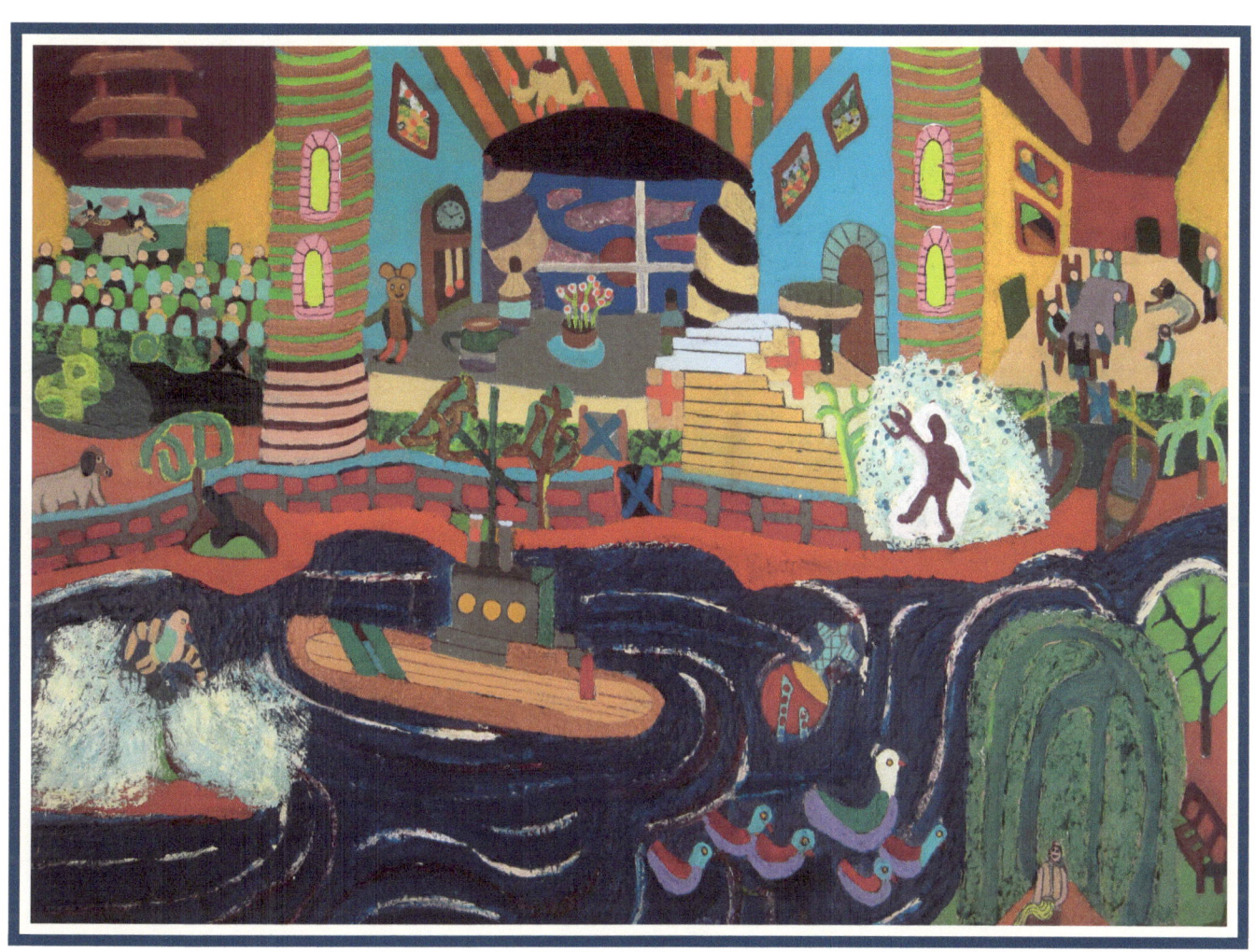

The Lazy Sailor. Mixed media.

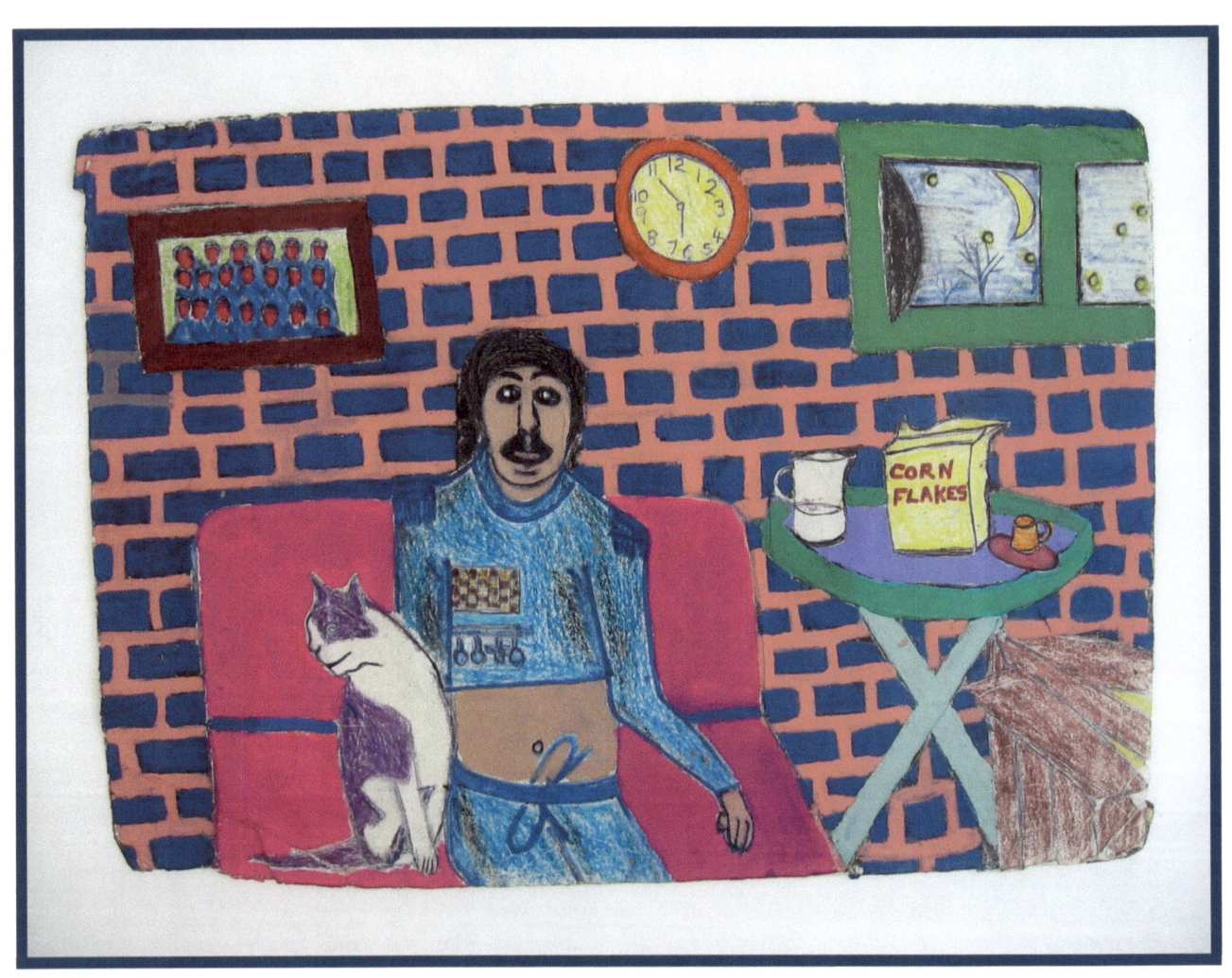

The Gentleman, Scholar, Painter and Decorator. Mixed media

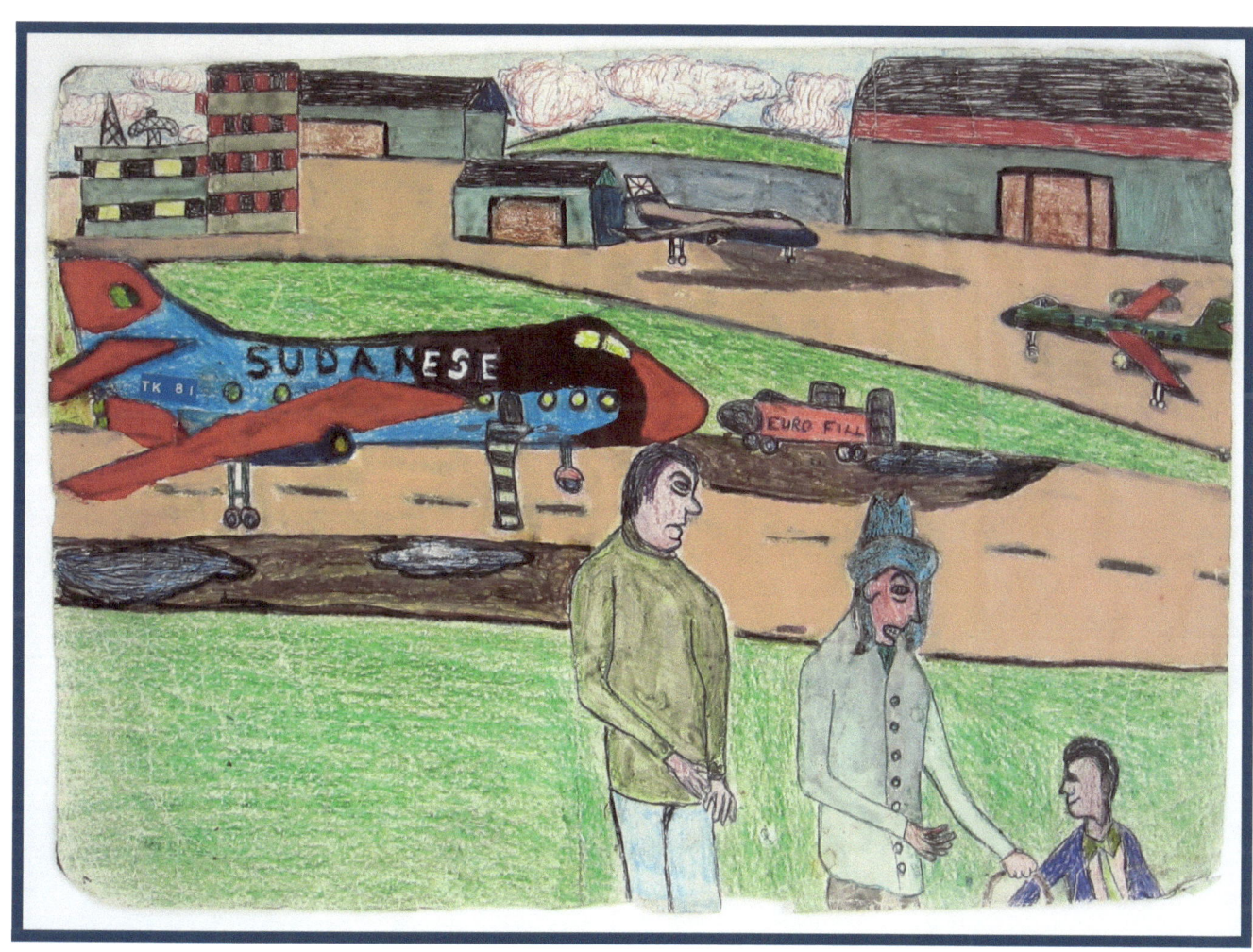

Before Going back to Prep School. Mixed media.

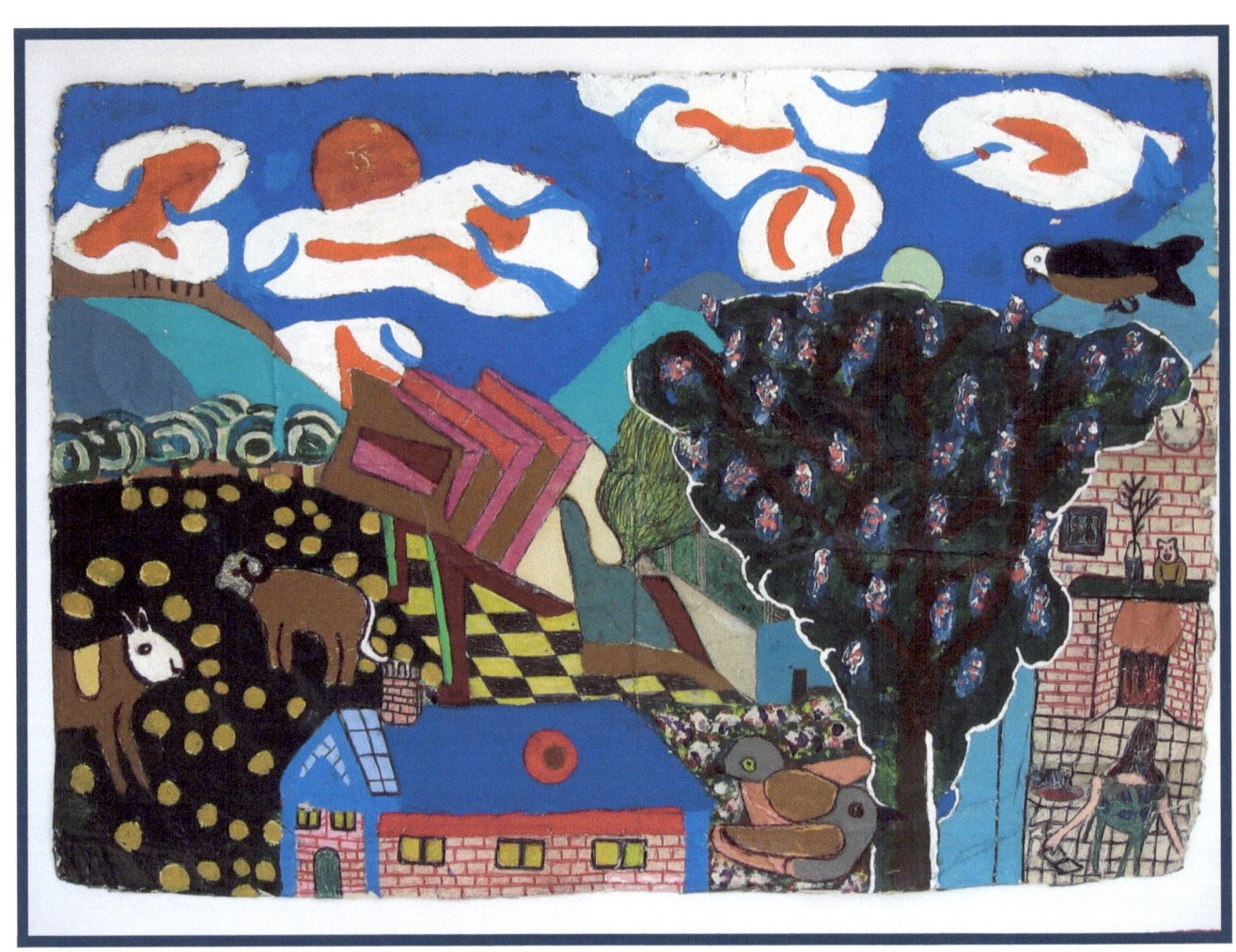

Neonic Social Commentary. Mixed media.

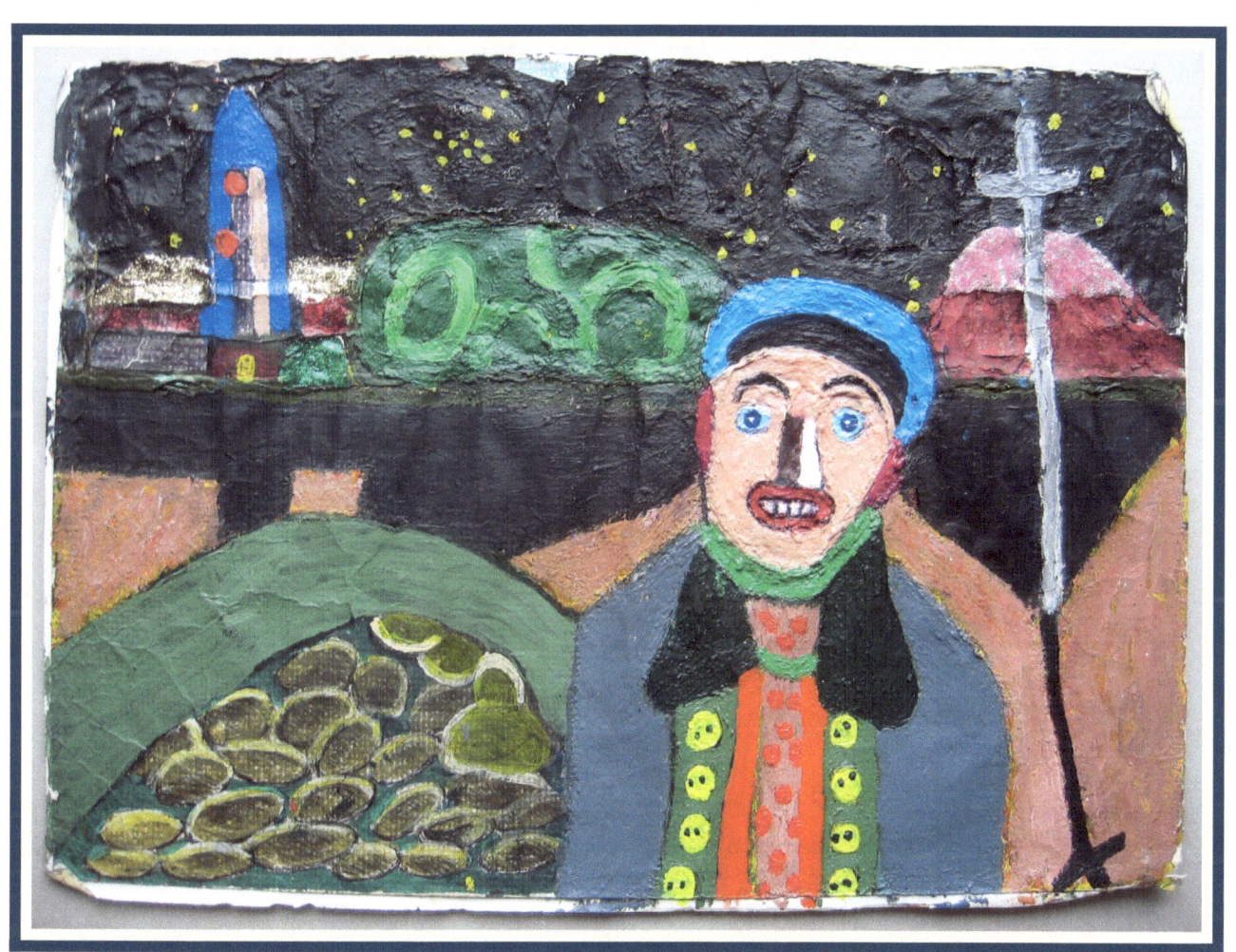

The Irishman They Knew. Mixed media.

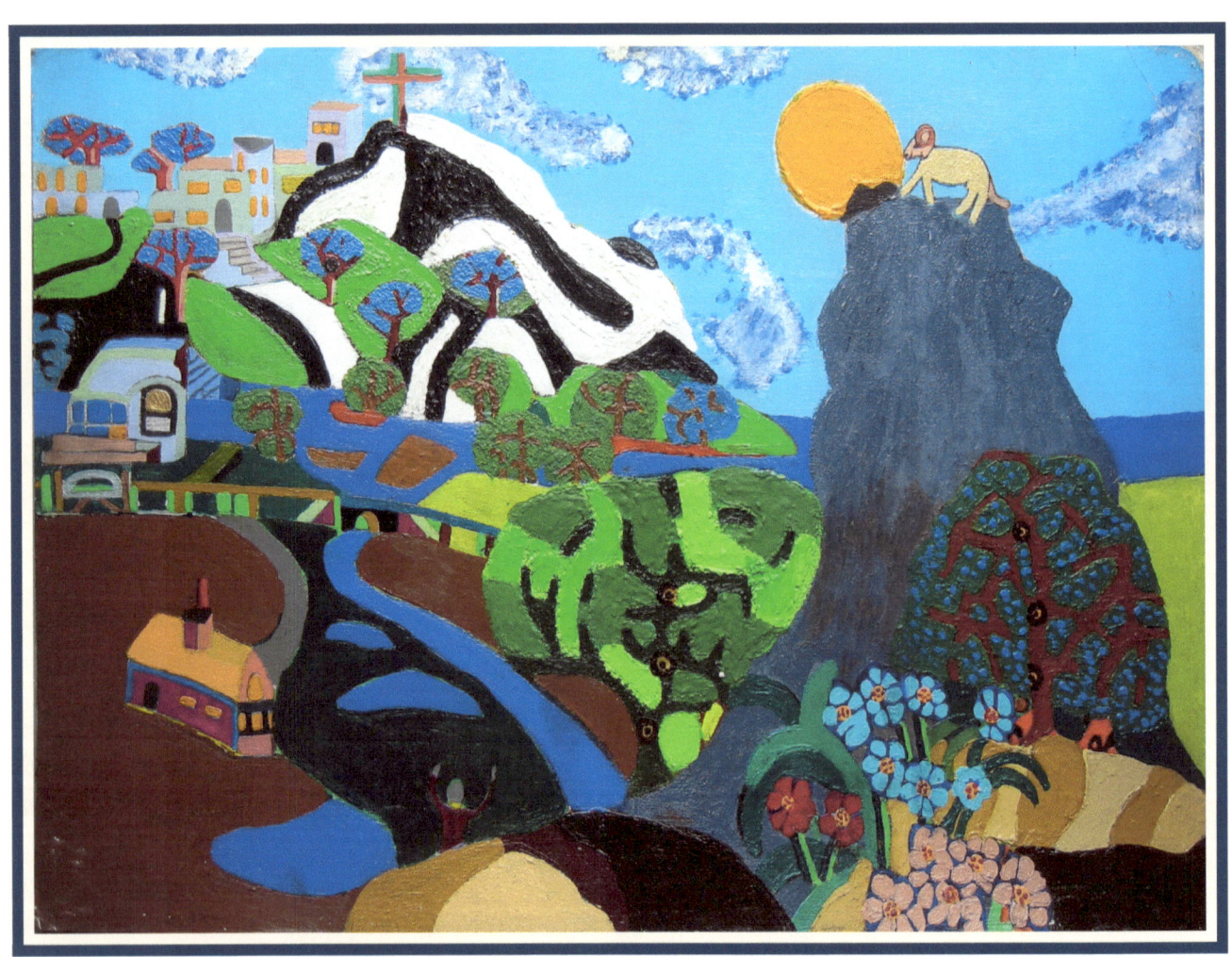

Far From the Madding Crowd. Mixed media.

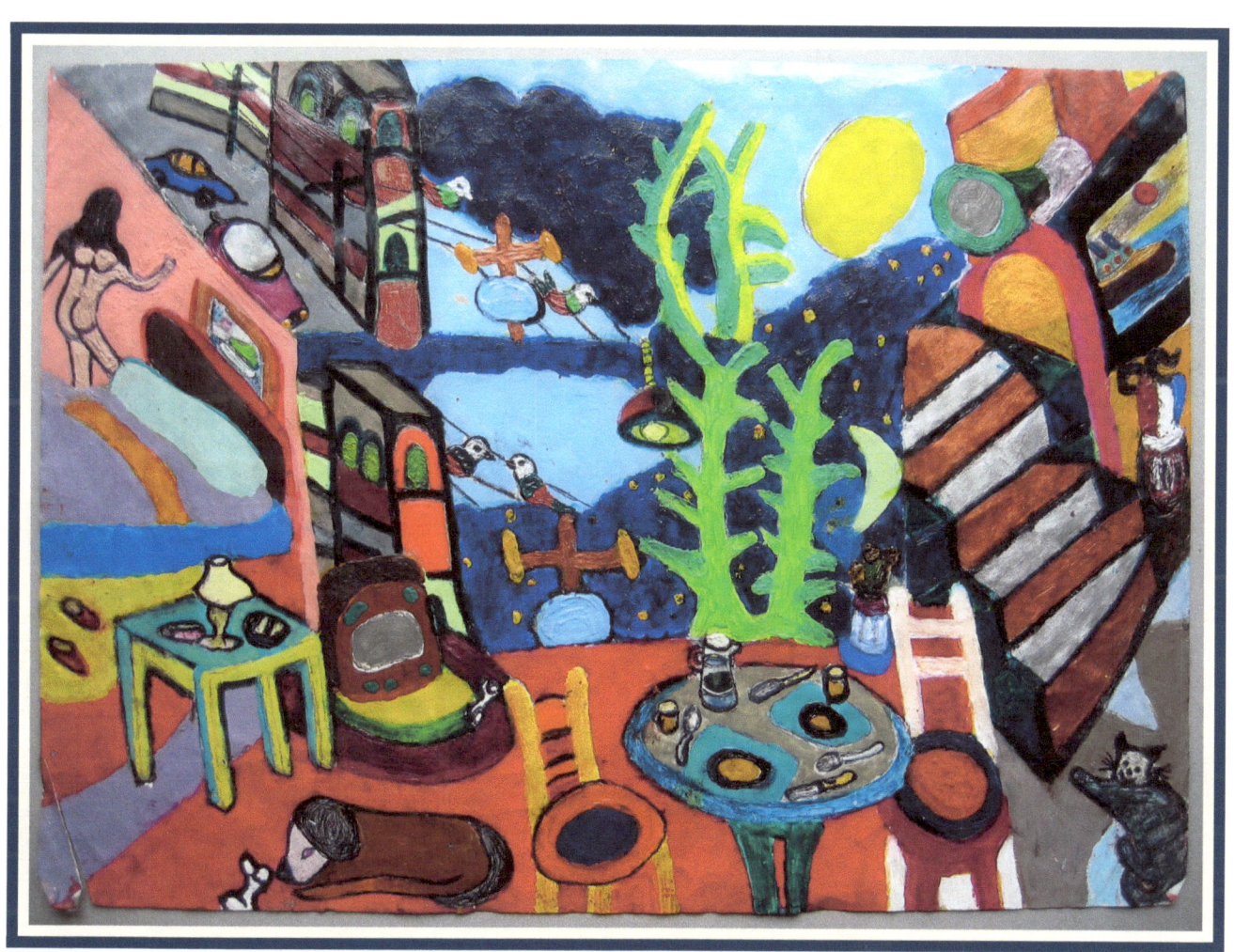

A Day in the Box . Mixed media.

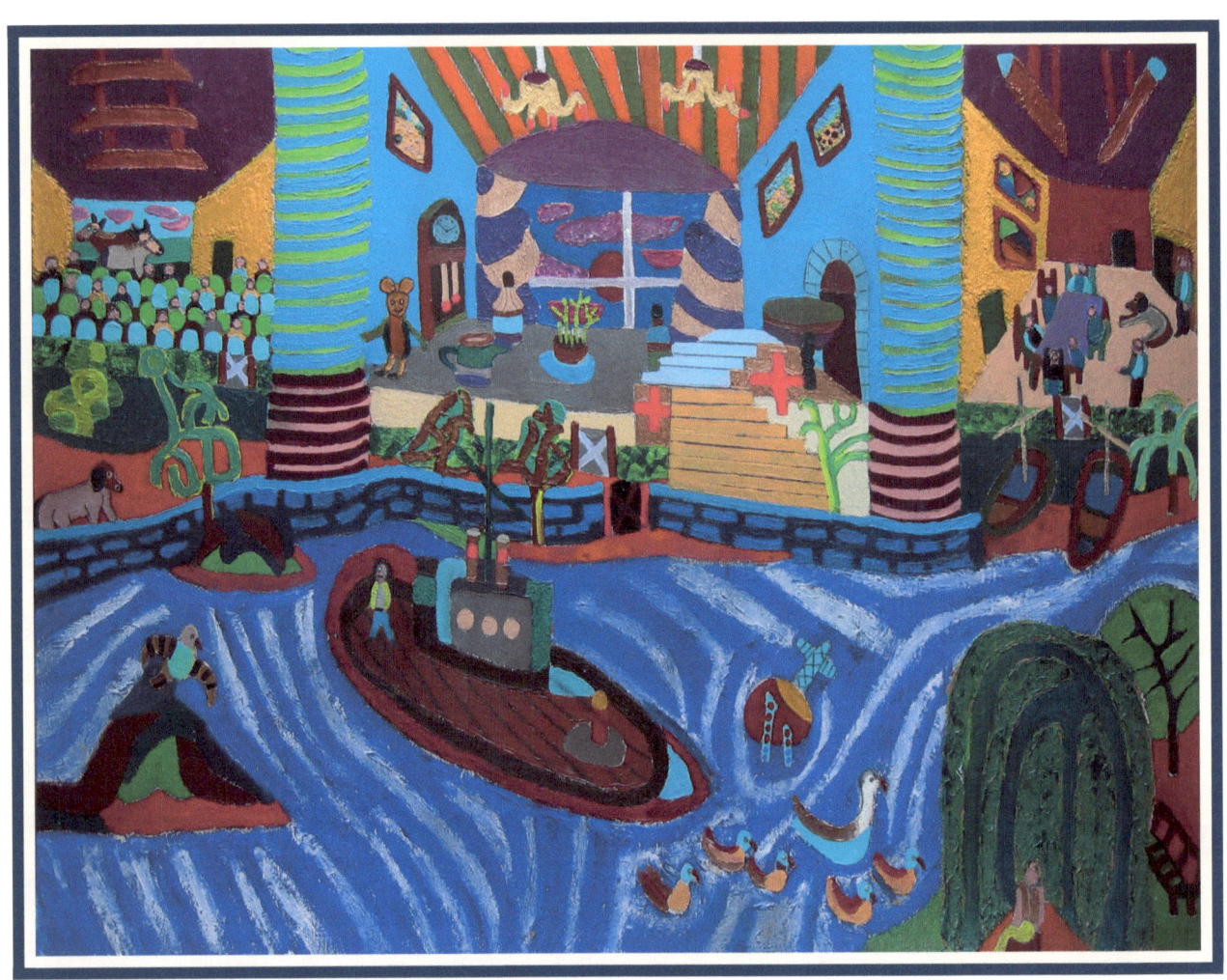

Crazy Sailor. Mixed media.

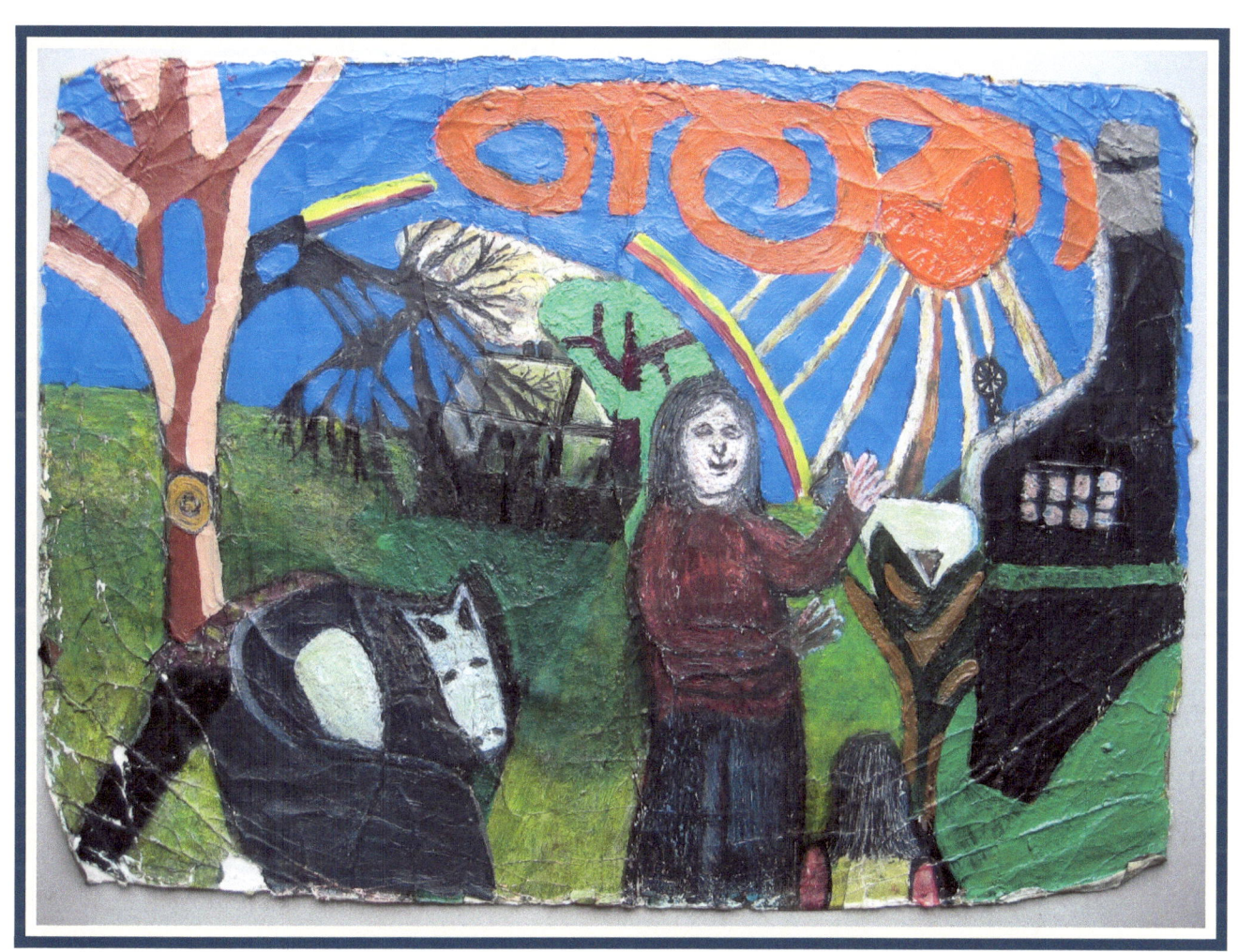

Dark Satanic Mills and the New England. Mixed media.

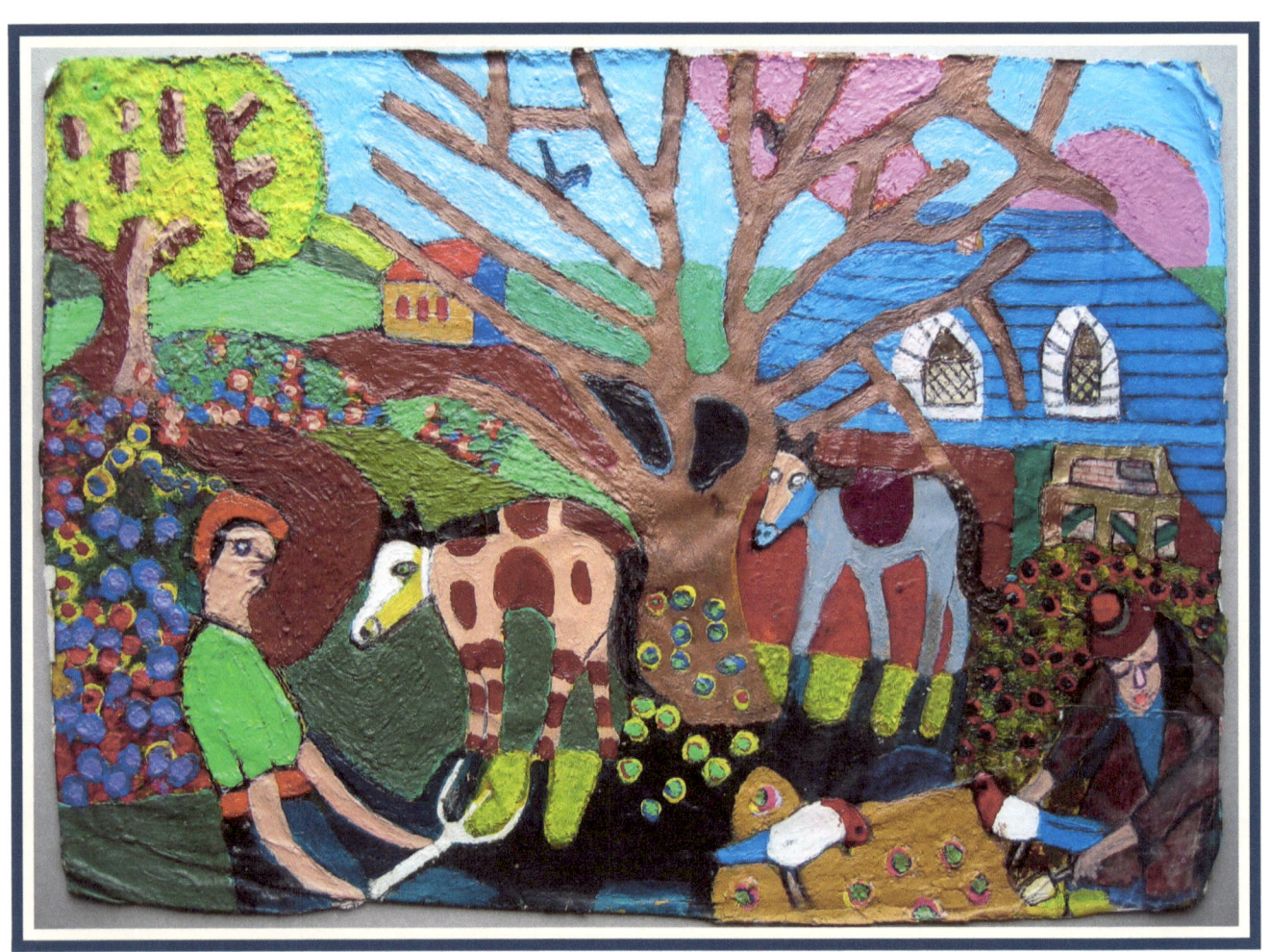

The Garden the Couple Wanted. Mixed media.

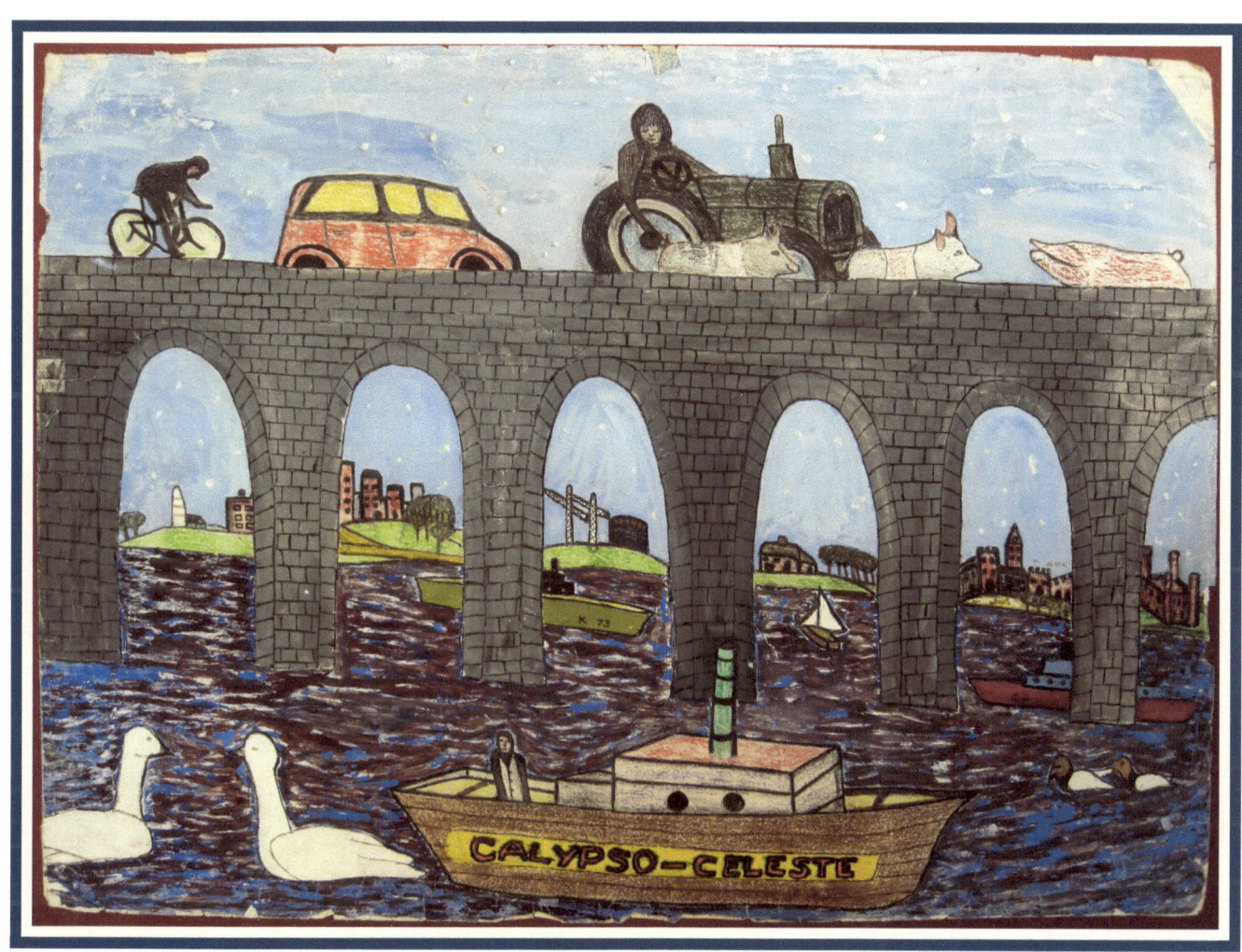

Pigs That Don't Fall in the Water. Mixed media.

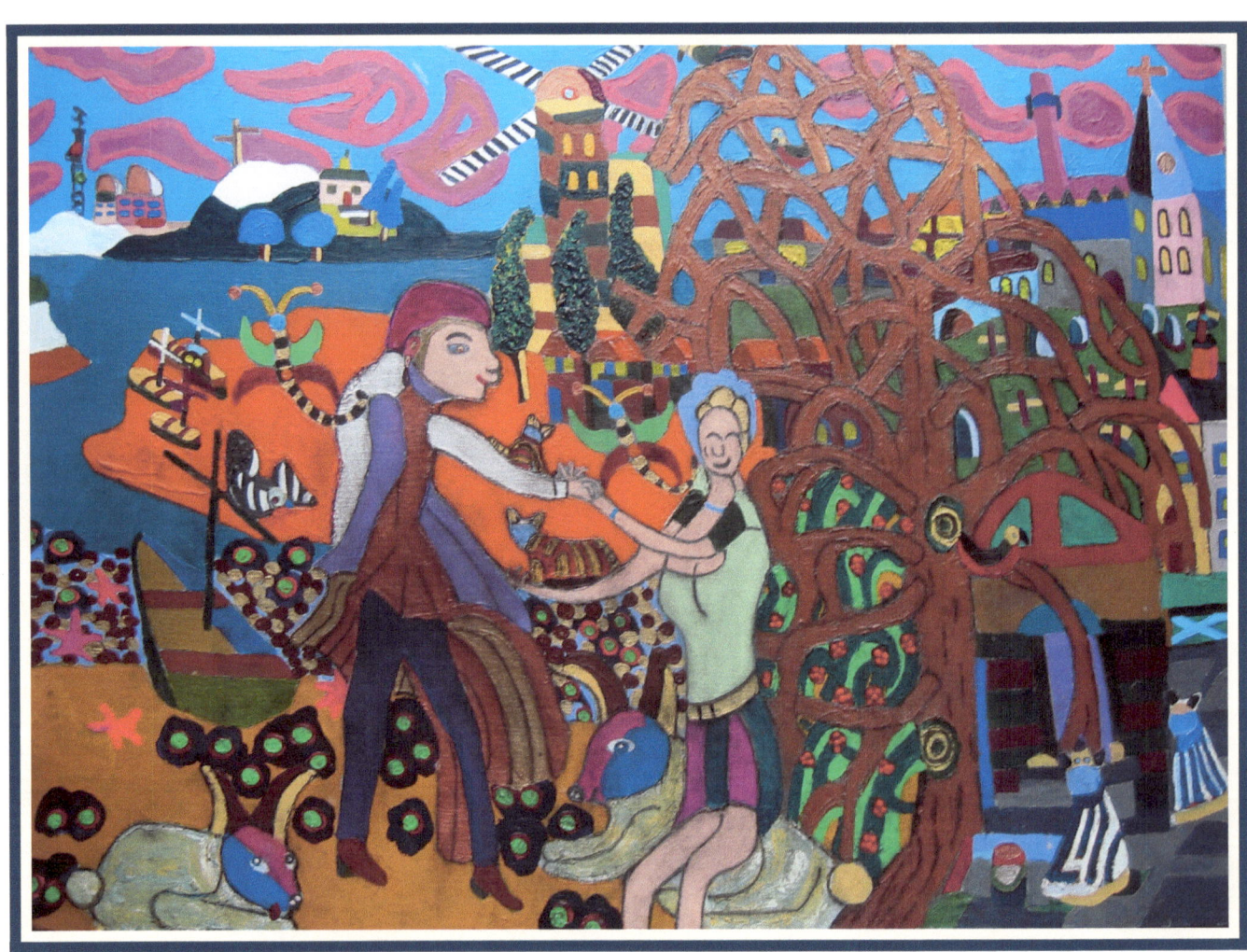

Mark and his Zoology Class. Mixed media.

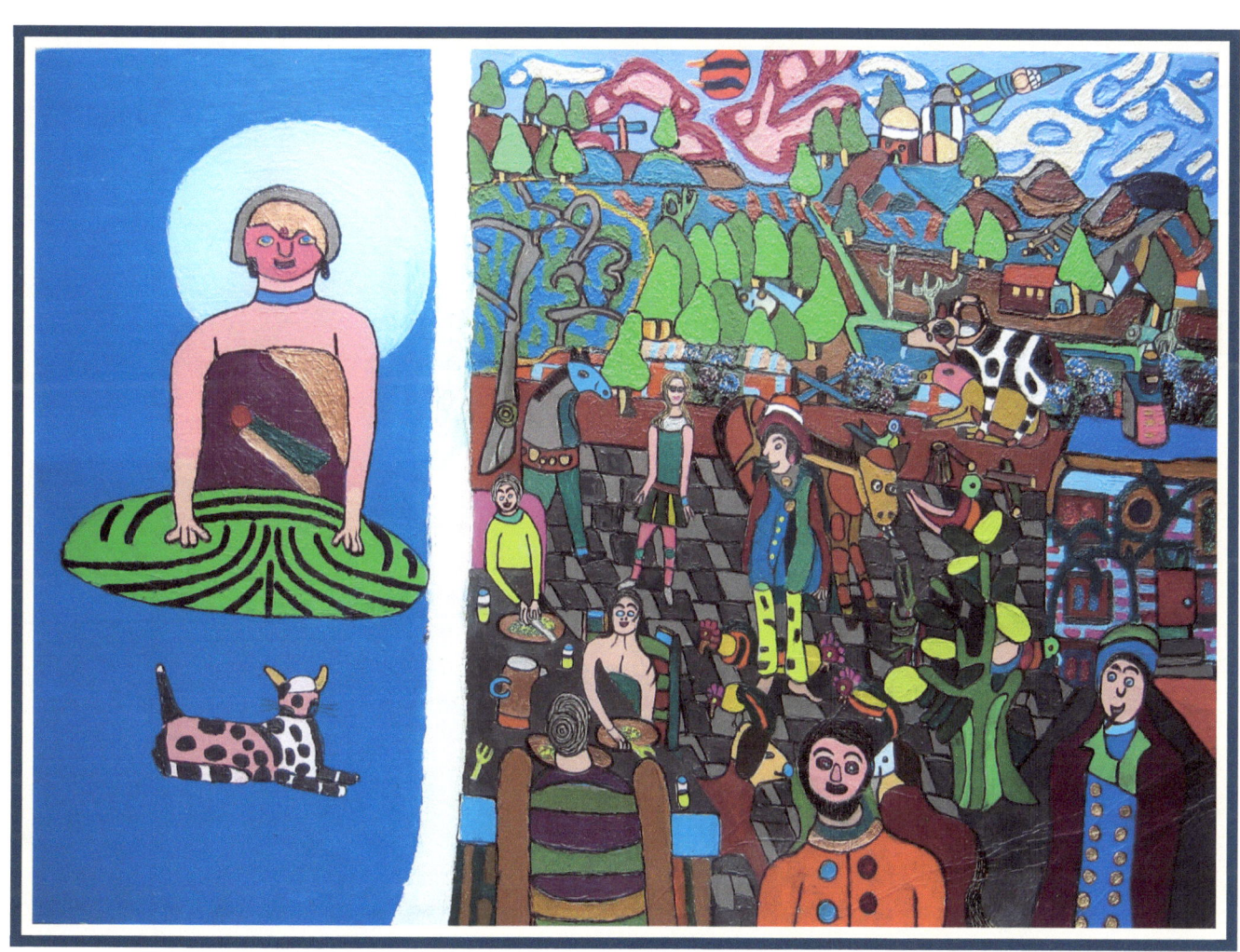

Friends of Buddha. Mixed media.

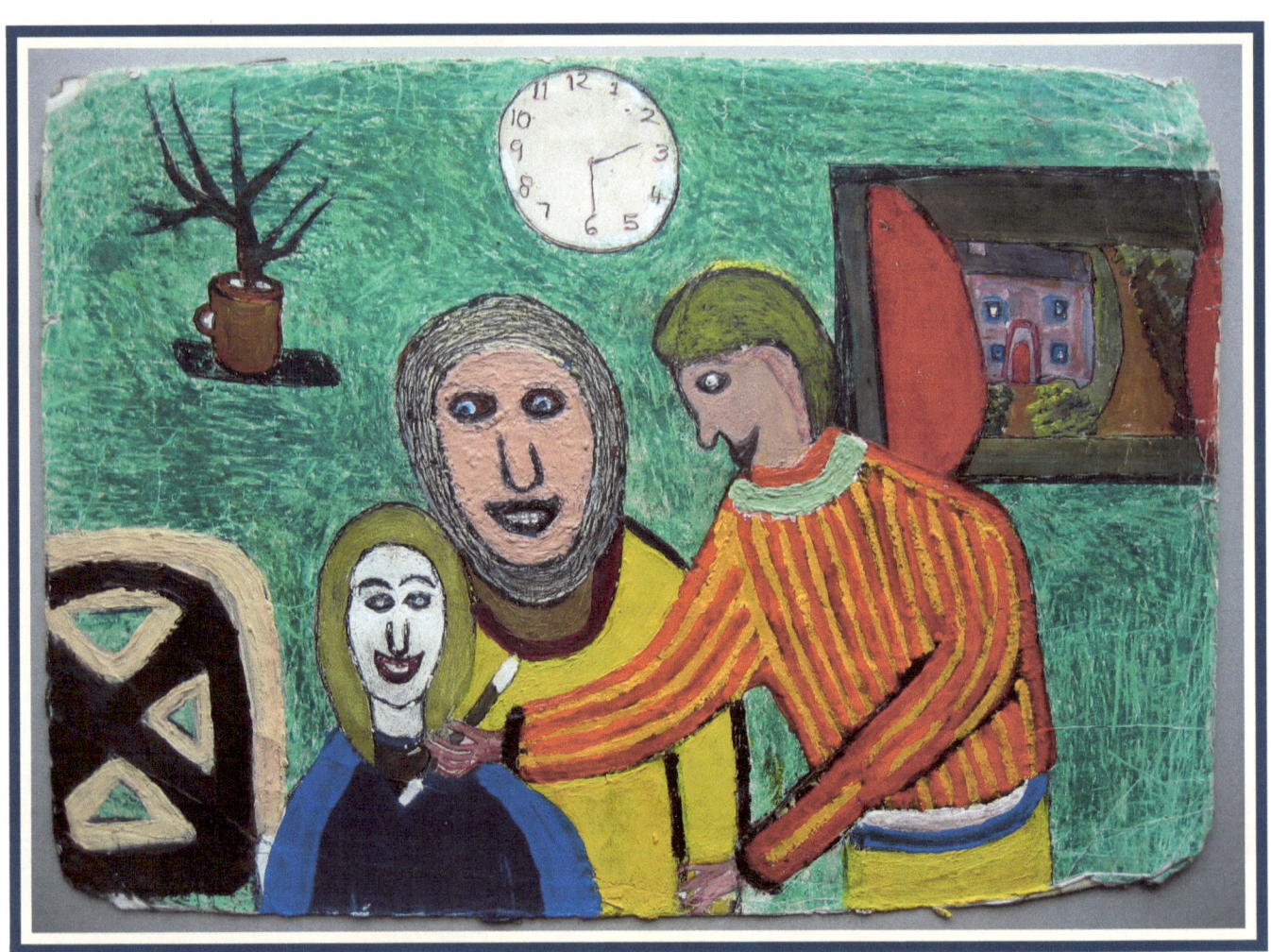

The Decision Among Friends. Mixed media.

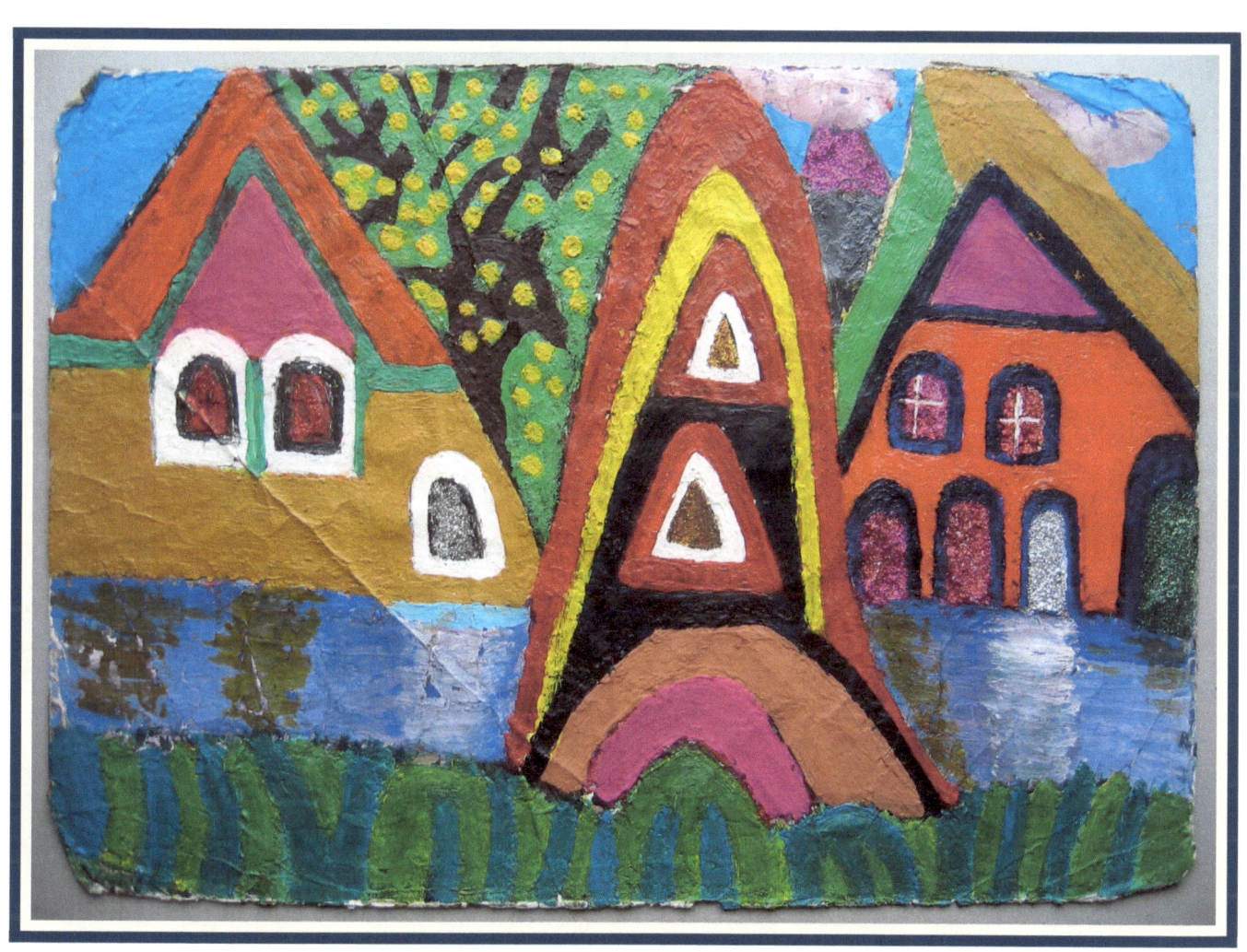

The Art Illusion. Mixed media.

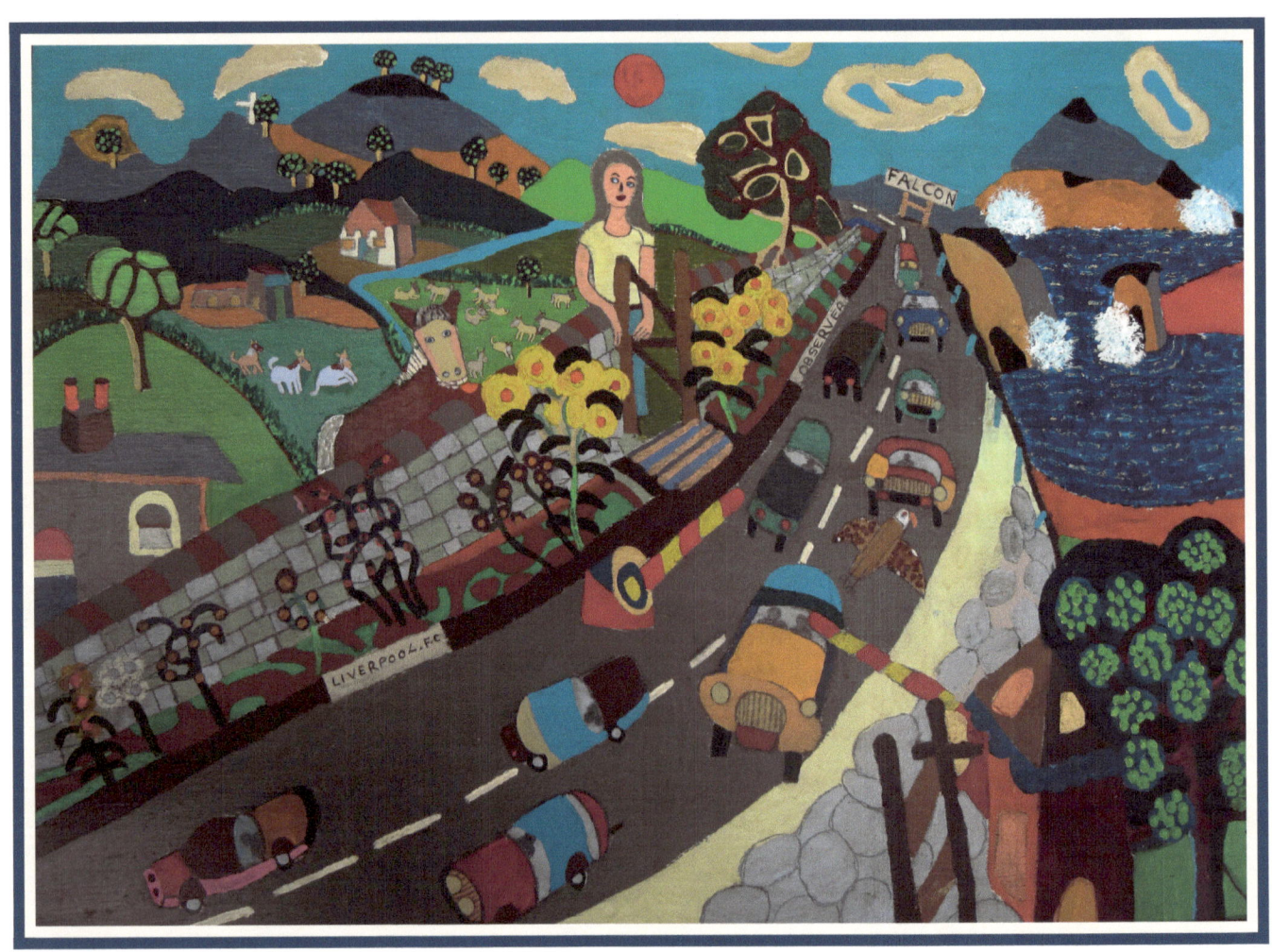

Geographic Event. Mixed media.

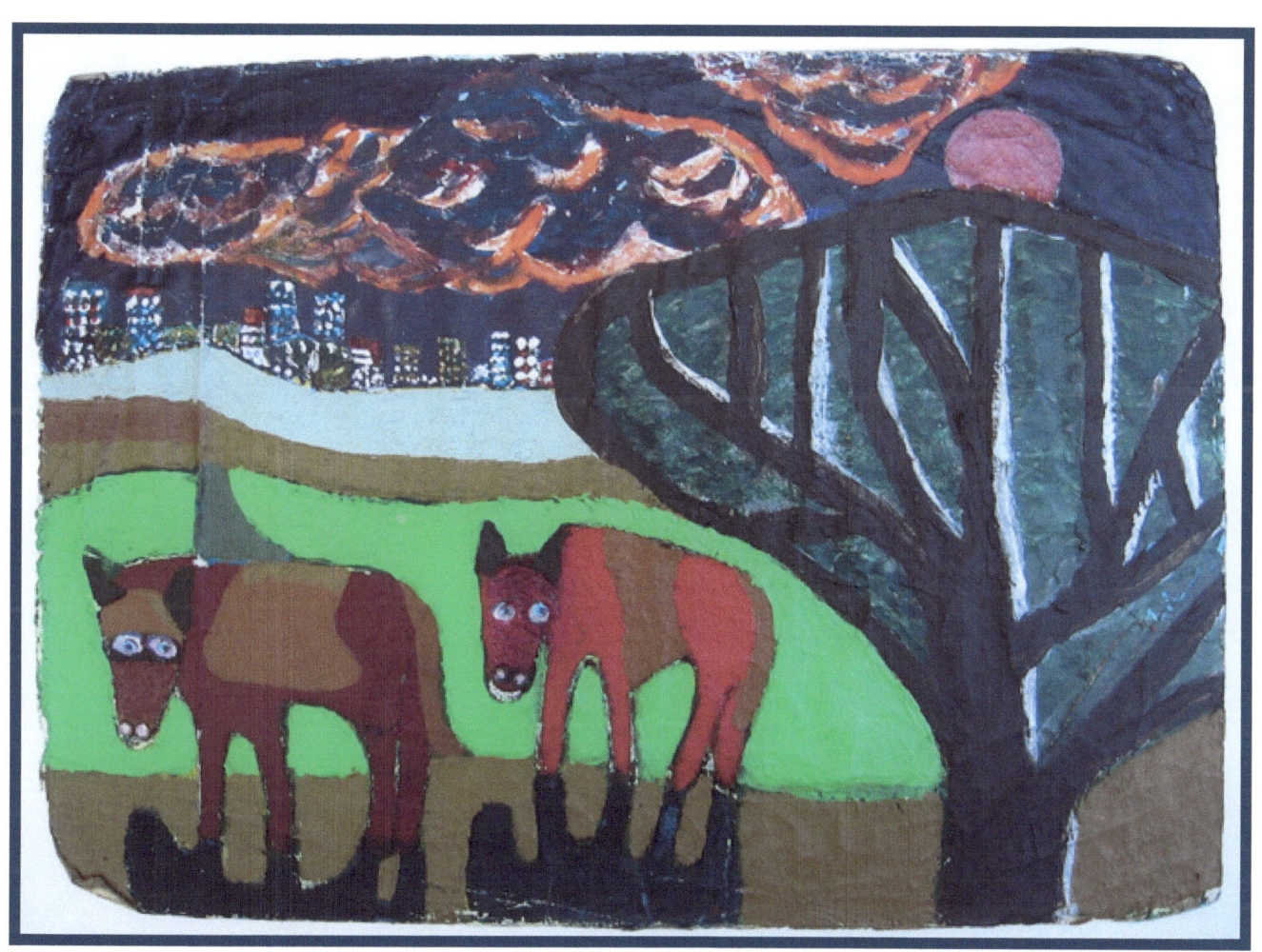

What Do We Do Next? Mixed media.

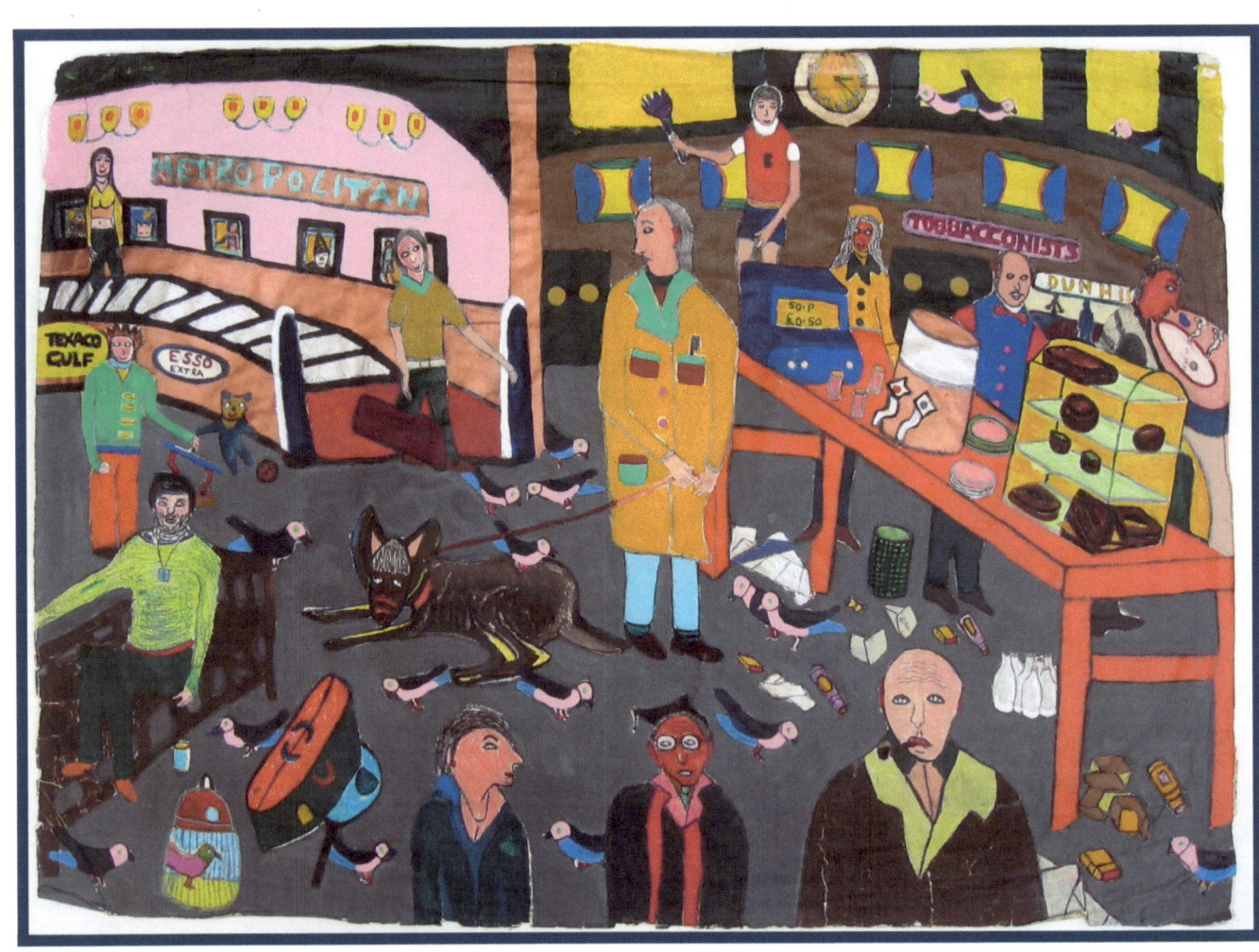

A Favorite Knuckle Sandwich. Mixed Media

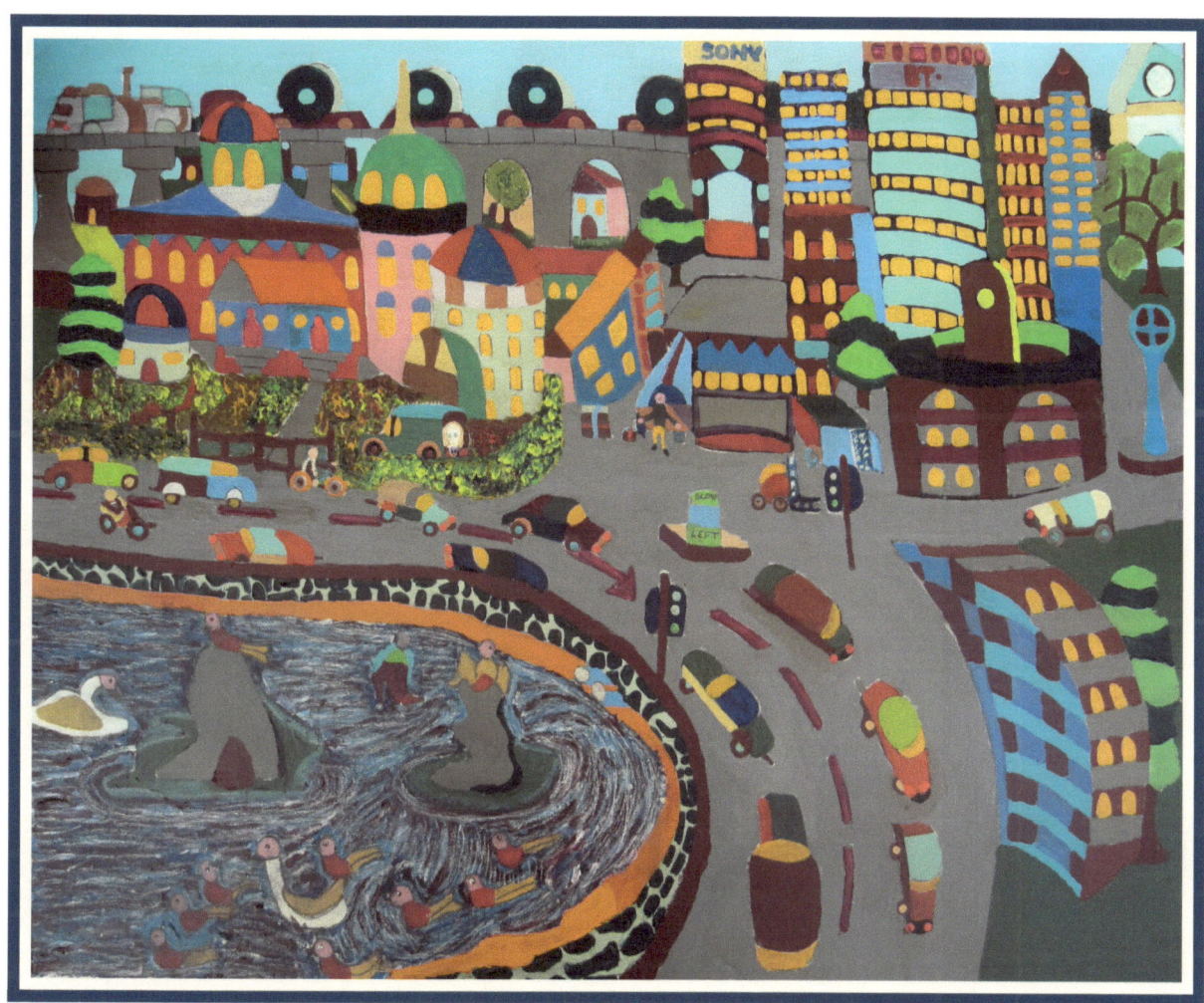

Urban Precinct. Mixed media.

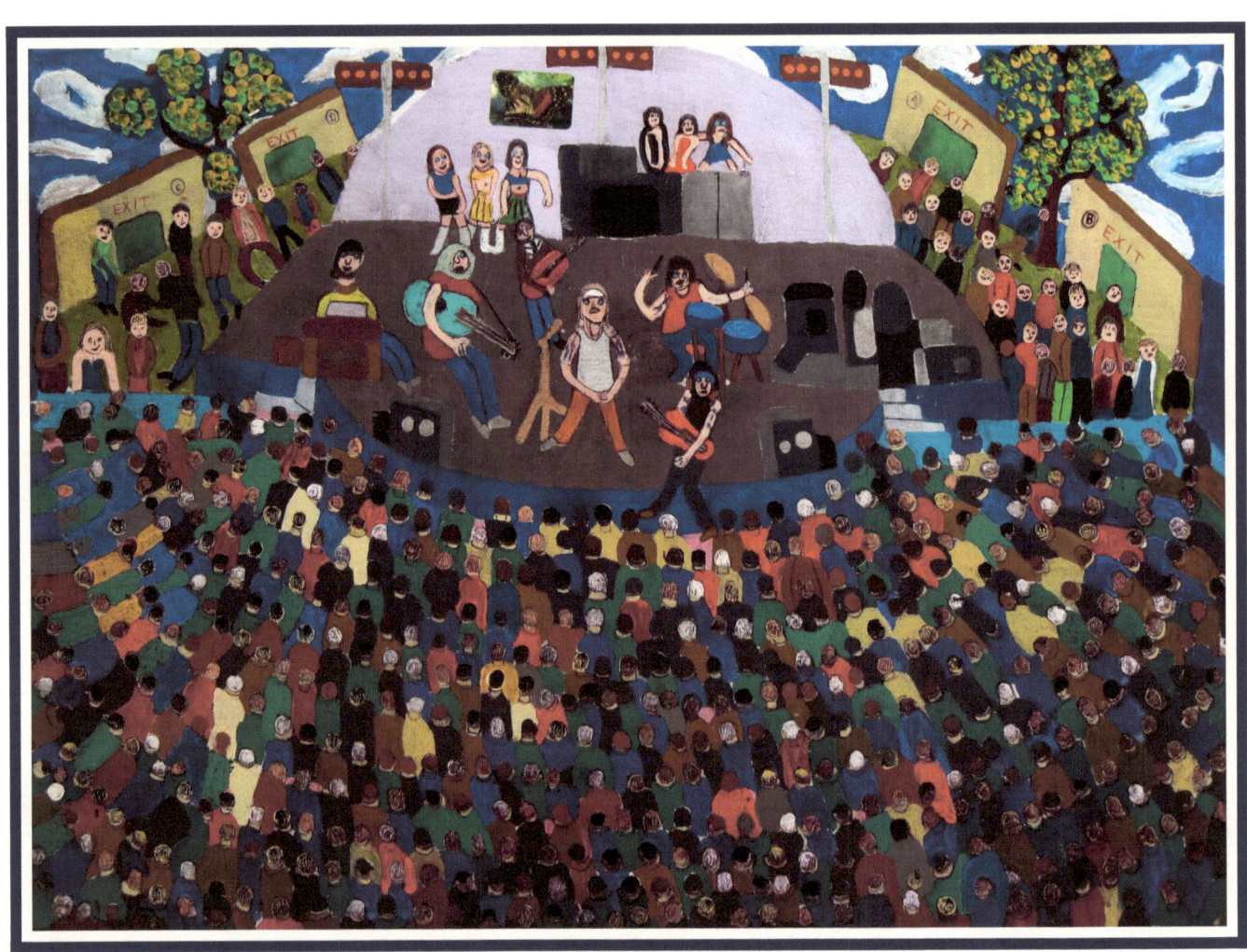

Gigoletrix and the Mir-cats. Mixed media.

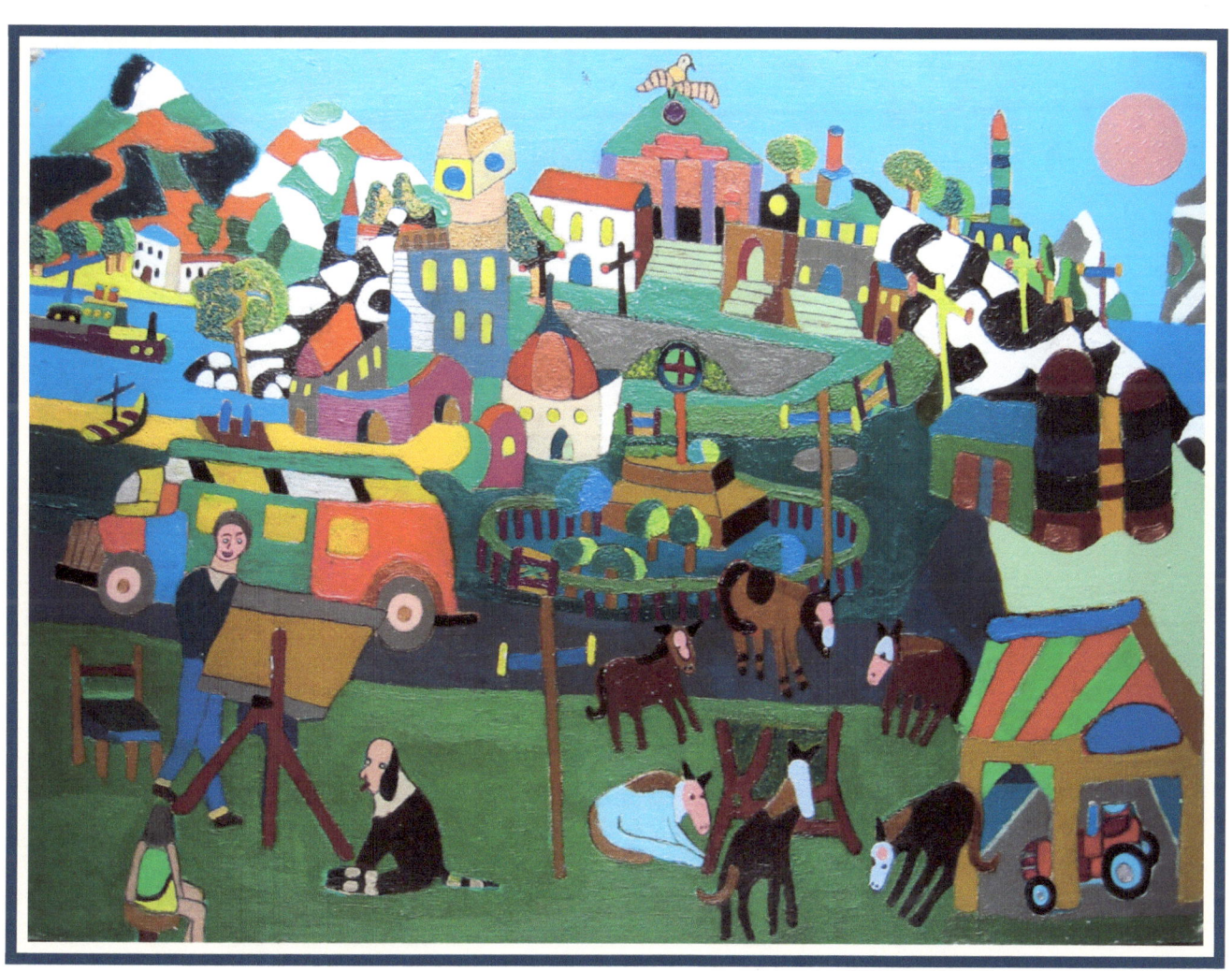

The Dock of the Bay. Mixed media.

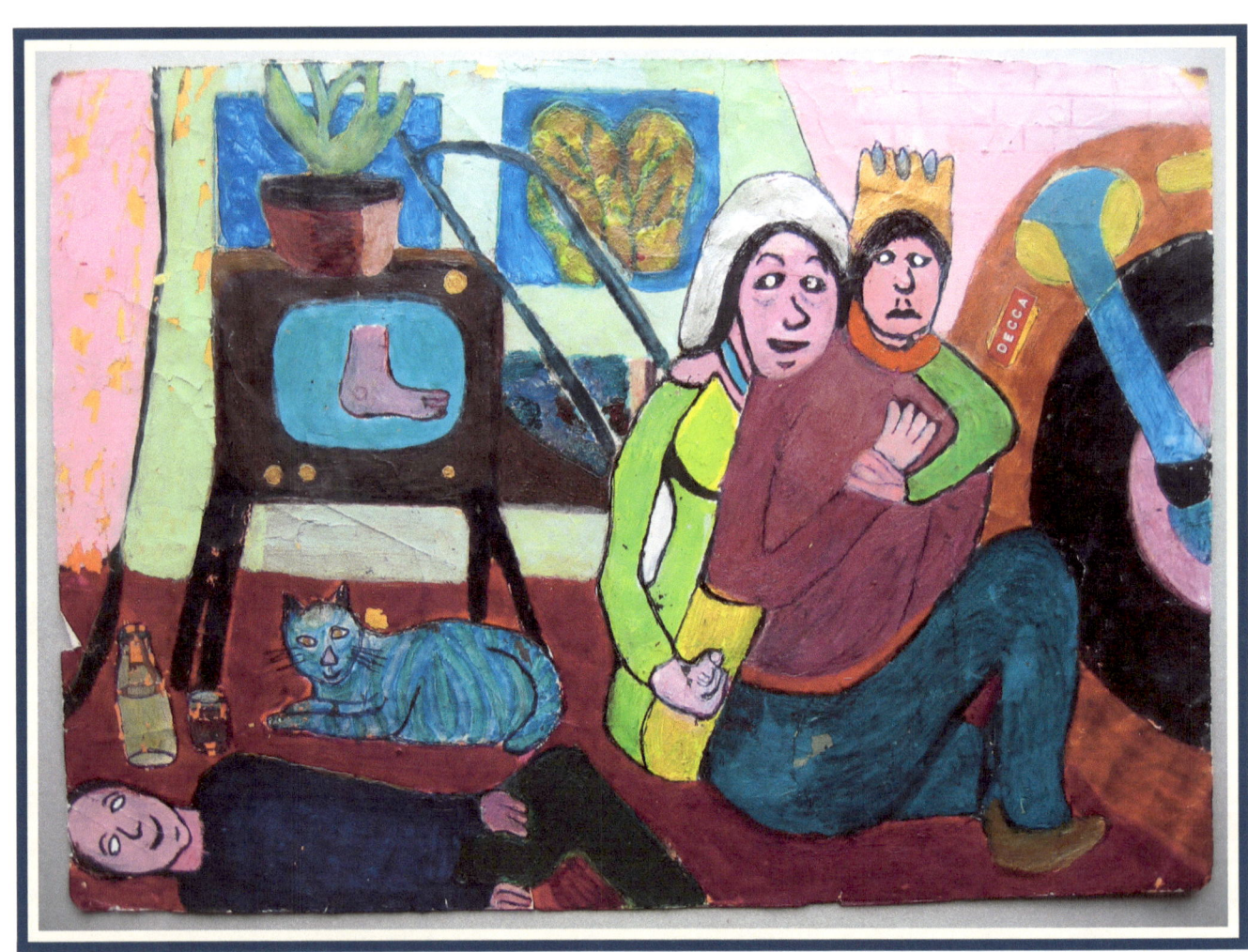

A Man for All Seasons & His Book, The Converted Self. Mixed media.

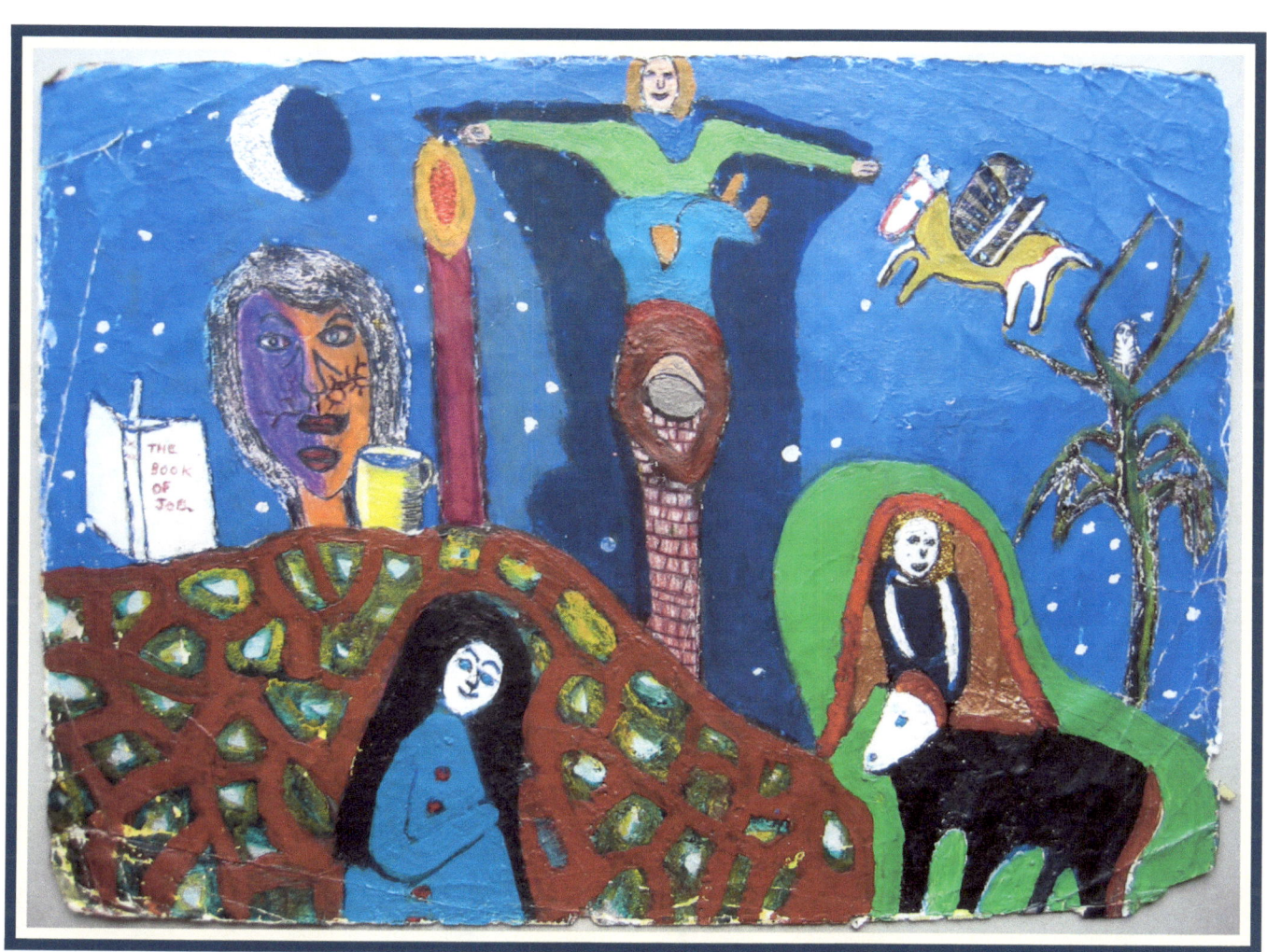

The Mistaken Jew. Mixed media.

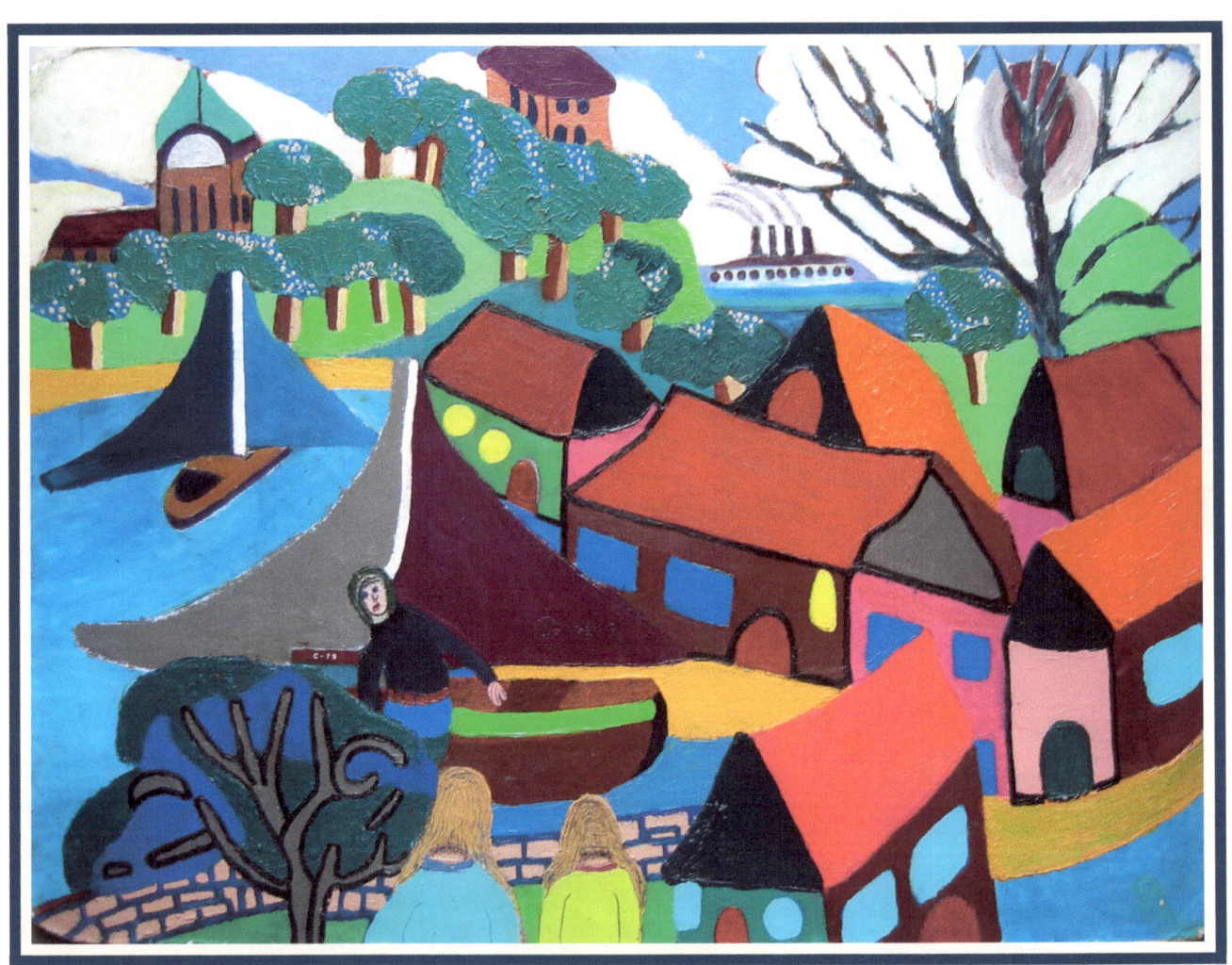

The Ship Coming In. Mixed media.

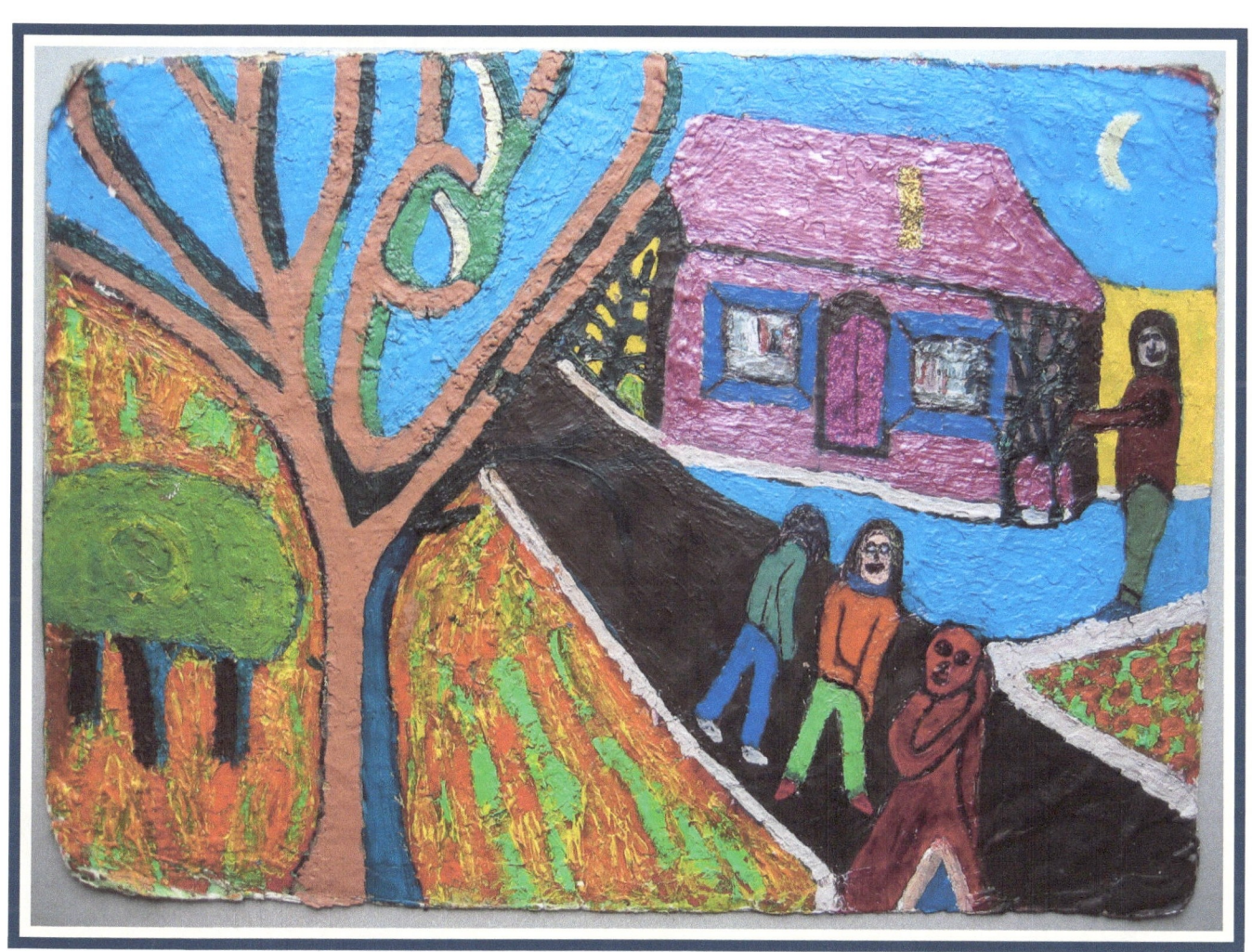

The Deed of Covenant. Mixed media.

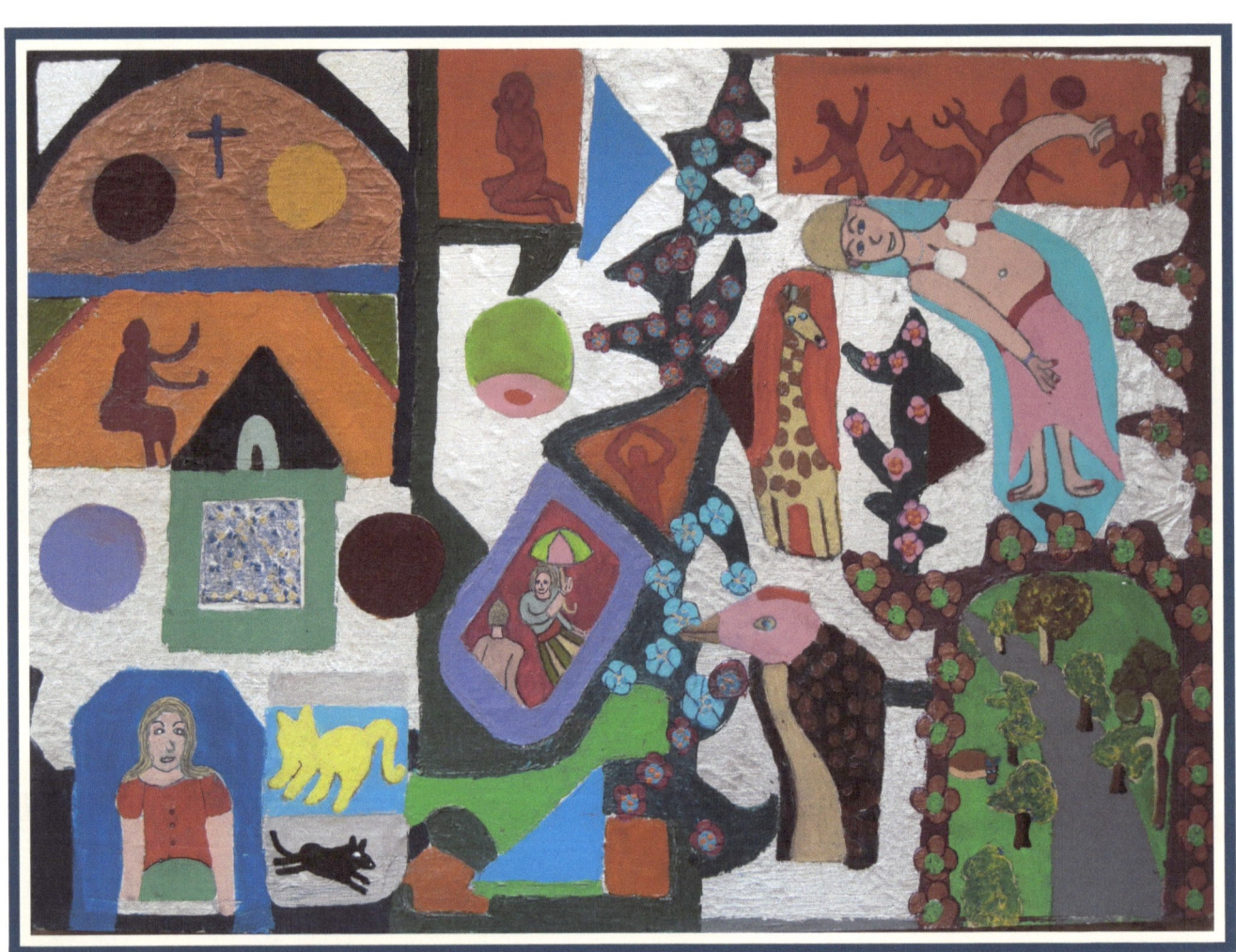

By Looking from the Ridge. Mixed media.

Thanks and Acknowledgements

Jenny Henriques.

Veronica Gosling - www.gallery36.co.uk

Staff at Caraston Hall

Cover, layout and design © Karen Huckvale. Insider Art 2012

Photographs by Malcolm Learmonth & Karen Huckvale

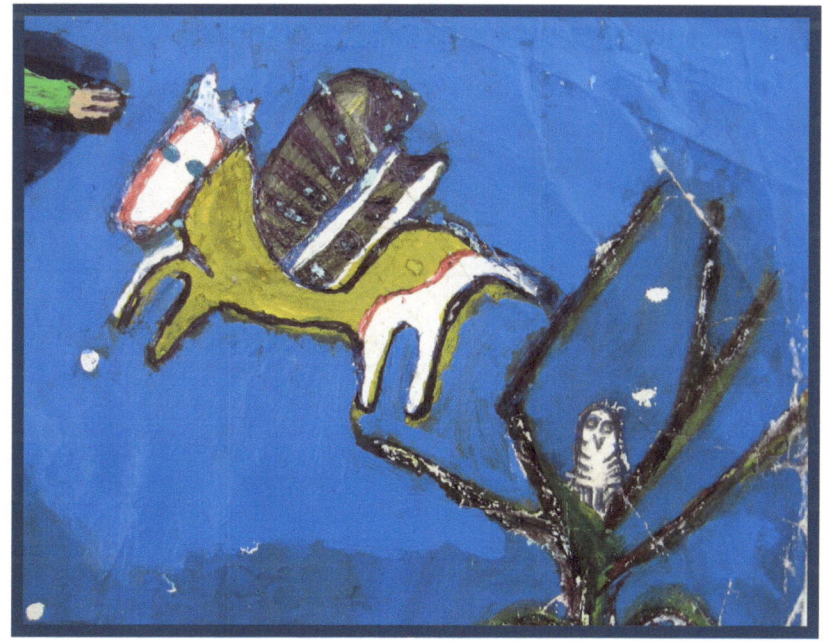

Detail: The Mistaken Jew

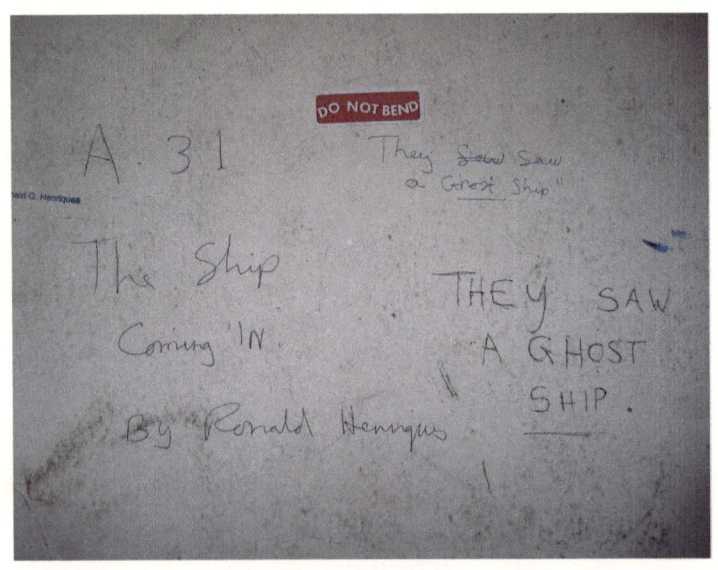

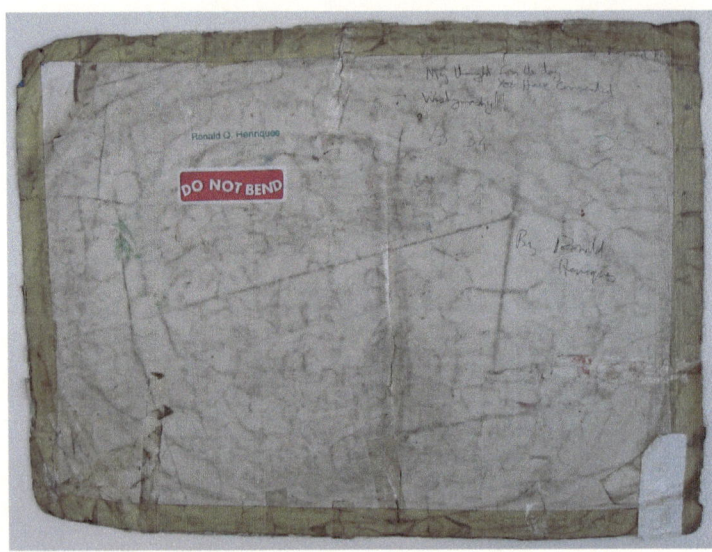

Reverse of paintings.